Advancing the Early Childhood Profession

NAEYC Standards and Guidelines for Professional Development

Alison Lutton, Editor

National Association for the Education of Young Children
Washington, DC

naeyc®

National Association for the
Education of Young Children
1313 L Street NW, Suite 500
Washington, DC 20005-4101
202-232-8777 • 800-424-2460
www.naeyc.org

NAEYC Books

Interim Editor in Chief
Derry Koralek

Director of Creative Services
Edwin C. Malstrom

Senior Editor
Holly Bohart

Design and Production
Malini Dominey

Assistant Editor
Elizabeth Wegner

Editorial Assistant
Ryan Smith

Permissions
Lacy Thompson

Cover photo copyright © by Ellen B. Senisi

Advancing the Early Childhood Profession:
NAEYC Standards and Guidelines for Professional Development

Copyright © 2012 by the National Association for the Education of Young Children. All rights reserved. Printed in the United States of America.

Library of Congress Control Number: 2011945900

ISBN: 978-1-928896-81-4

NAEYC Item #364

Contents

About This Volume

NAEYC first published guidelines for professional preparation programs in 1981. Those guidelines were organized into separate publications, one for four- and five-year programs (1981) and another for associate-degree granting institutions (1984). During the subsequent 30 years of periodic revision, NAEYC has organized these standards in a variety of ways. They were first collected and published in book form in 1996. In 2003 they were again published as one book with separate sets of associate, initial, and advanced standards.

NAEYC guidelines for program characteristics underwent substantive revision in 2001 with a shift to performance-based standards that measure program quality primarily through the assessment of program graduates. With the 2009 revisions, the NAEYC position statement became one statement of core professional performance standards, creating a unified framework for all early childhood professional development work. Accreditation materials for each degree level were published separately.

This newest volume of what has become known as the "red book" is designed as a resource for the entire early childhood field, across all early childhood professional roles and settings. It organizes the NAEYC position statements that describe what every early childhood professional should know and be able to do (the core professional preparation standards and Code of Ethical Conduct) and presents them alongside NAEYC documents that support states as they build professional development systems.

The 2010 NAEYC Standards for Initial & Advanced Early Childhood Professional Preparation Programs used by associate, baccalaureate, and graduate degree programs seeking NAEYC accreditation or recognition are published separately and available in PDF form at www.naeyc.org/accreditation.

Alison Lutton

Introduction

NAEYC has a long history of convening leaders in the field to develop the national guidelines and standards that have defined our profession over the past 80 years.

This book compiles current contributions to that continuing work and discussion. Taken together, these documents offer a road map for those of us who are engaged in our own professional development; in the development, implementation, and evaluation of training, education, and technical assistance programs; and in the development, implementation, and evaluation of state and national early childhood professional development systems.

Professional preparation standards as a vision for our profession

One of the hallmarks of a profession is that it has developed consensus around a common core body of knowledge and a code of ethical practice that is shared by all of its members. Standards for delivery of programs for young children began in 1929 with the NAEYC (then known as NANE—the National Association for Nursery Education) publication of *Minimum Essentials for Nursery School Education*. A core body of knowledge for the profession was first established in the early 1970s when NAEYC and a national consortium of organizations established the essential competencies required to earn the Child Development Associate (CDA) credential.

That common core body of knowledge was further developed in the 1981 NAEYC *Early Childhood Teacher Education Guidelines for Four- and Five-Year Programs* and the 1985 *Guidelines for Early Childhood Education Programs in Associate Degree Granting Institutions*, both of which embraced the structure of the CDA competencies. At the same time, the National Council for Accreditation of Teacher Education (NCATE) adopted the NAEYC standards as the national standards for recognition of early childhood teacher education programs in NCATE-accredited schools of education. The first NAEYC National Institute for Early Childhood Professional Development was held in 1991, accompanied by a series of articles in *Young Children* that explored key issues related to building professional development systems. The NAEYC standards for professional preparation were revised in 1996 and 2001. In 2006, NAEYC launched the Commission for Early Childhood Associate Degree Accreditation. In 2011, a session at the NAEYC National Institute for Early Childhood Professional Development celebrated 30 years of national standards for early childhood professional preparation and the first 100 accredited associate degree programs. The standards were most recently revised in 2009.

This book is organized into two parts. Part I presents the professional standards and code of ethics for all members of the early childhood profession and a supplement for those who provide professional development to adults. Part II presents guidance for the design and delivery of early childhood professional systems.

Part I includes

1. 2009 NAEYC Standards for Early Childhood Professional Preparation Programs

2. NAEYC Code of Ethical Conduct and Statement of Commitment

3. Supplement for Early Childhood Adult Educators

Together, the standards and Code of Ethical Conduct serve as a guide for the design, evaluation, and implementation of professional preparation and development programs, as well as a road map for individual professional development.

Effective professional practice requires effective professional development systems

Every profession has the responsibility to build systems that can ensure that its core body of knowledge is shared with all members of the profession, regularly reviewed and revised as needed, passed on to future generations, and integrated into the policies and systems that support the delivery of high-quality programs for young children. As stated by NAEYC staff in a contribution to the recently published *Pre-K Debates*, "In no profession is degree completion alone sufficient to ensure high-quality practice. Teacher quality is built, sustained, and increased through career-long professional development with attention to deliberate recruitment of candidates with promise, early experiences that inform and build commitment to the profession, successful degree program completion, and workplace-embedded training, coaching, and peer collaboration" (Willer et al. 2011, 82).

Part II of this book offers a road map for development of effective early childhood professional development systems. Part II includes

1. Workforce Designs: A Policy Blueprint for State Early Childhood Professional Development Systems

2. Early Childhood Education Professional Development: Training, Technical Assistance, and Early Childhood Education Glossary

3. Using the New NAEYC Professional Preparation Standards

Workforce Designs: A Policy Blueprint for State Early Childhood Professional Development Systems, the first document in this section, outlines four principles for policy making and six essential policy areas that must be addressed. As stated in the blueprint, "To be effective, each of these policies must be integrated, attending to all early care and education sectors; include quality assurance mechanisms; and support diversity—each incorporating the cornerstones of the policy-making principles" (Lemoine 2008, 12–13).

The second document in Part II, the *Early Childhood Education Professional Development: Training, Technical Assistance, and Adult Education Glossary* offers definitions of common terms used in program development, implementation, and evaluation; in policy decisions and regulations; and in research and literature reviews. These documents were developed in collaboration with the National Association of Child Care Resource and Referral Agencies (NACCRRA) and the Alliance of Early Childhood Teacher Educators (itself a collaborative effort of the National Association of Early Childhood Teacher Educators and ACCESS – Associate Degree Early Childhood Teacher Educators).

The article *Using the New NAEYC Professional Preparation Standards*, first published in the March 2011 issue of *Young Children*, provides a summary of the revisions to our profession's core body of knowledge and skills from 1981 to 2009 and makes the case for standards integration across the child care, Head Start, and P-12 funding and regulatory sectors of our field. As this article points out, "Standards are just one essential component of the systems needed to support developmentally effective teaching and learning. Essential components include the following: Professional standards; accredited training and education programs; early childhood licensing and certification; induction, mentoring, and coaching; leadership in the early learning program; adequate resources and working conditions; ongoing professional development; and engagement in professional networks and associations" (Lutton 2011, 81).

Questions for the road ahead

After NAEYC launched the National Institute for Early Childhood Professional Development in 1991, we also published in *Young Children* the article "Of Ladders and Lattices, Cores and Cones: Conceptualizing an Early Childhood Professional Development System" by Sue Bredekamp and Barbara Willer. That article identified a set of goals that unite our field and issues that need further discussion and debate in order to strengthen the profession of early care and education (p. 49–50). Revisiting those goals and questions can help us to both recognize the work accomplished and envision the road ahead.

1. The 1992 article asked whether the belief that early childhood is a large and varied profession built upon a common core of knowledge is a valid one. "Are such different roles as home-based parent educator, center director, second grade teacher, early intervention specialist, or infant caregiver truly specialties built upon a common core, or are they separate but allied professions?"

   Over the past 20 years, we have continued to define and differentiate the roles that comprise our profession through both state and national work. A number of national organizations, including the National Association for Family Childcare and the McCormick Center for Early Childhood Leadership, have developed core knowledge and competencies for family child care providers, directors, and other specialized roles for professionals working with children from birth through age 8. Today there are more than 500 NAEYC-recognized associate, baccalaureate, and graduate degree programs offering preparation for work with children from birth through age 8. NAEYC and the Council for Exceptional Children/Division of Early Childhood work together to offer national recognition to "blended" preparation programs that meet the standards of these two separate but allied professions—early childhood education and special education. An emerging question is how to build professional development (PD) systems that bridge the developmentally based definition of the early childhood profession and location-based definitions of elementary school teachers and school-age child care providers.

2. A second question raised in 1992 was, "How [will] core content and specialty areas [be] translated into specific professional development programs? What should be taught to whom and when? . . . It will be important that states and other entities plan training programs that reflect core knowledge and are structured to be part of an overall system."

States have made much progress in this area of work. During the 1990s, a number of states engaged in the development of a core body of knowledge that could unify state early childhood training and education offerings. Some developed individual professional development records. State credentials, training registries, and quality rating and improvement systems soon followed. The majority of these used the NAEYC standards as a framework.

3. The 1992 article identified areas that must be addressed more effectively in our professional development systems, including cultural and linguistic diversity for full inclusion of children with exceptionalities; early childhood advocacy, curriculum, and assessment; and work with infants and toddlers.

These areas for improvement in our professional preparation programs have been repeatedly identified by research. Too few professional development programs have the capacity to keep up with current theory and research. Too few adequately prepare program completers for diversity, inclusion, and work with infants and toddlers. There are not enough degree programs available to provide initial preparation for the teachers we need and precious few graduate programs that provide advanced preparation for the early childhood teacher educators, researchers, program administrators, or policy analysts and advocates that we need.

4. In 1992, we pointed out that while career ladders are an important strategy to improve compensation and retention, they need to be accompanied by the concept of a career lattice that better "conveys the realities of the diverse settings, roles, and responsibilities in programs serving children from birth through age 8 . . . it also reflects goals that are not yet achieved: enhanced upward mobility with improved compensation and increased opportunity for horizontal movement from one sector to another."

This challenge remains critical today, with very little progress. State credentials rarely lead to meaningful improvements in compensation, unless the individual moves from the child care to the education sector of the field. And in the education sector, teacher salaries are generally not competitive with other professions that expect comparable levels of qualification and accountability.

Access to professional development and upward mobility has improved, but quality evaluation and improvement structures for professional development programs are not consistently implemented. It is possible to begin one's professional development with an online e-CDA that is sponsored by, and articulates into, an accredited online associate degree program, continue studies at an NAEYC-recognized bachelor program, and later return for an online NAEYC-recognized master's degree program. But online programs are not the answer for all learners. In some states all early childhood degree programs in public higher education institutions hold NAEYC accreditation or recognition. In others, there are none to be found.

*　　　*　　　*

New questions about state PD system coordination and capacity have emerged. How can we ensure that 50-plus different state and territory systems use the common core NAEYC standards and Child Development Associate (CDA) competencies? Without common national standards, how can credentials be portable across states and across the child care, Head Start, and education professional development systems within states? How can we ensure that state credentials are aligned with the two national early childhood credentials, the Child Development Associate certification for entry-level practitioners and the National Board Early Childhood Generalist Certification for accomplished teachers? Both the CDA and National Board credentials are aligned with the NAEYC standards for professional preparation, but not all states embrace these credentials and integrate them into their own systems. To build a truly portable credential, we also need to build national consensus around which positions are or should be comparable across settings.

How do we build the capacity of higher education programs and their field site partners to meet the needs of our professional development systems? Can we support and sustain accreditation systems and other strategies to support professional development programs that engage in effective self-study and ongoing improvement work on persistent areas of concern? The past few years have seen growth in NAEYC accreditation for associate degree programs and recognition for bachelor degree programs as mechanisms for continuous improvement and for demonstrating that teaching and learning in these professional preparation programs is aligned with national professional standards. In many states, higher education programs will need increased institutional and external support to build their capacity to meet state early childhood professional development goals.

Finally, in the past two decades, the need for a more diverse workforce has emerged as a new issue facing professional development systems, along with the need to learn more about effective professional development for linguistically and culturally diverse adults. The NAEYC decision to launch an associate degree accreditation system reflected the growth of associate degree programs in early childhood education and their importance in building professional pathways for diverse and nontraditional students. The 2009 NAEYC Position Statement on Standards for Early Childhood Professional Preparation Programs suggests that associate degree programs need to simultaneously offer substantive coursework that prepares graduates for professional roles in the field while keeping transfer doors open. All professional preparation and development programs need to be intentionally responsive to unique needs of their states, communities, and specific demographic groups of adult students. We know that our professional development and preparation programs need to improve and to change. Can national standards serve as a framework that supports innovation, creativity, diversity, and leadership development? We are exploring that question now with both opportunities and challenges ahead.

Closing

Each of the documents in this compilation is intended as a contribution to current discussions in the field about what early childhood professionals should know and be able to do, how to assess the quality of professional training and education programs, what constitutes a meaningful professional credential, and how to build effective systems that will attract and retain a skilled workforce with the compensation and professional development needed to sustain a long-term career.

Each was developed through a process of information gathering, input from individuals with relevant expertise and perspectives, and public comment on draft documents. NAEYC is grateful to the hundreds of people whose contributions make this compilation possible. Special acknowledgments are included with each document.

Two primary goals of an articulated system of professional development originally suggested in 1992 are worth renewed energy and focus twenty years later. First, "Every child—regardless of the setting—will have access to high-quality services that reflect professional knowledge," and second, "the current inequities in status and compensation among early childhood professionals will be corrected" (Bredekamp & Willer 1992, 50).

A word on NAEYC accreditation

Because this book is not focused on how to earn NAEYC accreditation or recognition, the full NAEYC accreditation and recognition standards are not included here. The core standards and key elements included in this book are comparable to the initial standards. The key elements of the advanced standards move more deeply into content and practice as applied in specific advanced roles such as accomplished early childhood teacher, adult educator, administrator, advocate, policy specialist, and researcher.

Degree programs that are housed in accredited institutions of higher education may be eligible for national accreditation or recognition from NAEYC. To earn national accreditation or recognition, these programs must

1. Provide evidence that learning opportunities and key assessments are aligned with NAEYC professional preparation standards

2. Provide aggregate data on student performance for each standard

3. Submit reports on use of that data to inform and improve teaching and learning

For detailed information on NAEYC accreditation of initial-level early childhood associate degree programs, recognition of initial baccalaureate programs, recognition of initial or advanced graduate programs, and recognition of blended early childhood and special education programs, please visit www.naeyc.org/accreditation.

References

Bredekamp, S., & B. Willer. 1992. Of ladders and lattices, cores and cones: Conceptualizing an early childhood professional development system. *Young Children* 47 (3): 47–50.

Copple, C., & S. Bredekamp, eds. 2009. *Developmentally appropriate practice in early childhood programs serving children from birth through age 8.* 3d ed. Washington, DC: NAEYC.

Lemoine, S. 2008. *Workforce designs: A policy blueprint for state early childhood professional development systems.* Washington, DC: NAEYC.

Lemoine, S., A. Lutton, D. McDonald & J. Daniel. 2011. Integrating professional standards for the early childhood workforce: Putting the pieces together. In *Foundations for teaching excellence: Connecting early childhood quality rating, professional development, and competency systems in states*, eds. C. Howes & R.C. Pianta, 47–67. Baltimore, MD: Brookes.

Lutton, A. 2009. NAEYC early childhood professional preparation standards: A vision for tomorrow's early childhood teachers. In *Conversations on early childhood teacher preparation: Voices from the working forum for teacher educators*, eds. A. Gibbons & C. Gibbs, 29–36. Redmond, WA: World Forum Foundation; Auckland: New Zealand Tertiary College.

Lutton, A. 2011. Professional development. Using the new NAEYC professional preparation standards. *Young Children* 66 (2): 78–82.

NAEYC. 2009. *NAEYC standards for early childhood professional preparation programs.* Position Statement. Washington, DC: Author. Online: www.naeyc.org/files/naeyc/file/positions/ProfPrepStandards09.pdf

NAEYC. 2011. *Code of ethical conduct and statement of commitment.* Position Statement. Washington, DC: Author. Online: www.naeyc.org/files/naeyc/file/positions/Ethics%20Position%20Statement2011.pdf

NAEYC. 2011. *Code of ethical conduct: Supplement for early childhood adult educators.* Position Statement. Washington, DC: Author. Online: www.naeyc.org/files/naeyc/file/positions/ethics04.pdf

Willer, B., A. Lutton & M. Ginsberg. 2011. The importance of early childhood teacher preparation: The perspectives and positions of the National Association for the Education of Young Children. In *The pre-k debates: Current controversies & issues*, eds. E. Zigler, W. Gilliam & S. Barnett, 77–83. Baltimore, MD: Brookes.

PART I

Becoming an Early Childhood Professional

NAEYC Standards for Early Childhood Professional Preparation Programs

Code of Ethical Conduct and Statement of Commitment

Code of Ethical Conduct
Supplement for Early Childhood Adult Educators

Contents

NAEYC Standards
for Early Childhood Professional Preparation Programs

Approved by the NAEYC Governing Board July 2009

Introduction

The purpose of this position statement

NAEYC Standards for Early Childhood Professional Preparation Programs represents a sustained vision for the early childhood field and more specifically for the programs that prepare the professionals working in the field. This 2009 revision of the standards is responsive to new knowledge, research and conditions while holding true to core values and principles of the founders of the profession. It is designed for use in a variety of ways by different sectors of the field while also supporting specific and critical policy structures, including state and national early childhood teacher credentialing, national accreditation of professional early childhood preparation programs, state approval of early childhood teacher education programs, and articulation agreements between various levels and types of professional development programs.

History

NAEYC has a long-standing commitment to the development and support of strong early childhood degree programs in institutions of higher education. NAEYC standard setting for degree programs in institutions of higher education began more than 25 years ago. This document is the third revision to NAEYC's Early Childhood Teacher Education Guidelines for Four- and Five-Year Programs (1982) and Guidelines for Early Childhood Education Programs in Associate Degree Granting Institutions (1985).

Development and publication of those first standards documents was made possible through the contributions of family and friends of Rose H. Alschuler, a founding member and first Secretary-Treasurer of NAEYC from 1929-1931. During the 1920s, Ms. Alschuler was an early proponent and director of the first public nursery schools in the United States. During the 1930s she directed Works Progress Administration (WPA) public nursery schools in Chicago. During World War II she chaired the National Commission for Young Children. Her life and legacy continue today as our field furthers its work to improve both programs for young children and programs that prepare early childhood professionals.

The revisions process

The 1985 guidelines for preparation of early childhood professionals were revised in 1996, 2001-2003, and again with this revision in 2009. Each of these

...elines and standards was developed
...t from hundreds of early childhood profes-
...who participated in conference sessions,
...ory committees, and work groups. While these
...position statements of NAEYC, each was developed with invited input from colleagues in related
professional associations, including ACCESS—early
childhood educators in associate degree granting institutions, the National Association of Early
Childhood Teacher Educators (NAECTE), the
Division for Early Childhood of the Council for
Exceptional Children (CEC/DEC), and the National
Board for Professional Teaching Standards
(NBPTS).

In January 2008, NAEYC's Governing Board
appointed a working group to advise staff on the
preparation of a revision of the current *Preparing
Early Childhood Professionals: NAEYC's Standards
for Programs* (2003). This work group was composed of early childhood faculty members from
associate, baccalaureate, and graduate degree
programs; representatives of NAEYC, ACCESS, and
NAECTE; and faculty who use the standards in
the National Council for Accreditation of Teacher
Education (NCATE) and NAEYC Early Childhood
Associate Degree Accreditation (ECADA) systems. Additional input into the standards revi-
sion process was gathered during sessions at
the 2007 NAEYC Annual Conference, the 2008
NAEYC Public Policy Forum, and the 2008 NAEYC
National Institute for Early Childhood Professional
Development. Draft revisions were posted on the
NAEYC Web site for public comment in Fall 2008.
Final revisions were completed in Spring 2009.

What is new?

From all of these perspectives, the feedback indi-
cated that the standards remain strong. Revisions
called for are primarily organizational and reflect
input from those who are actively implementing
the standards in the field. There are *two* significant
revisions in this 2009 document.

1. Standard 4 has been separated into two standards,
   one focuses on early childhood methods and the
   other on early childhood content. This increases
   the total number of standards from five to six.

2. The language *all children* is revised to read
   either *each child* or *every child* to strengthen the
   integration of inclusion and diversity as threads
   across all standards. In some cases, the phrase
   "each child" has been added to a key element of
   a standard.

Like all NAEYC position statements, the standards
for early childhood professional preparation are
living documents and as such will be regularly
updated and revised.

Standards as a vision of excellence

With good reason, many educators have become
wary of standards. At times, standards have con-
stricted learning and have encouraged a one-size-
fits-all mentality. But standards can also be vision-
ary and empowering for children and professionals
alike. NAEYC hopes its standards for professional
preparation can provide something more valuable
than a list of rules for programs to follow.

The brief standards statements in this document offer a shared vision of early childhood
professional preparation. But to make the vision
real, the details must be constructed uniquely and
personally, within particular communities of learners. Good early childhood settings may look very
different from one another. In the same way, good
professional preparation programs may find many
pathways to help candidates meet high standards,
so that they can effectively support young children
and their families. (Hyson 2003, p. 28)

Unifying themes for the field

These standards express a national vision of excellence for early childhood professionals. They are
deliberately written as statements of core knowledge, understanding, and methods used across
multiple settings and in multiple professional roles.
The key elements of each standard progress from
a theoretical knowledge base to more complex
understanding to the application of knowledge in
professional practice.

These 2009 NAEYC Standards for Early
Childhood Professional Preparation Programs
continue to promote the unifying themes that
define the early childhood profession. These standards are designed for the early childhood education profession as a whole, to be relevant across
a range of roles and settings. These core NAEYC
standards are for use across degree levels, from
associate to baccalaureate to graduate degree programs. They are used in higher education accreditation systems, in state policy development, and
by professional development programs both inside
and outside institutions of higher education.

These core standards can provide a solid, commonly held foundation of unifying themes from

which diverse programs may arise, incorporating the wisdom of local communities, families, and practitioners. These unifying themes include

- **Shared professional values,** including a commitment to diversity and inclusion; respect for family, community, and cultural contexts; respect for evidence as a guide to professional decisions; and reliance on guiding principles of child development and learning.

- **Inclusion of the broad range of ages and settings** encompassed in early childhood professional preparation. NAEYC defines early childhood as the years from birth through age 8. These standards are meant to support professional preparation across diverse work settings, including infants and toddlers, primary grades, family child care, early intervention, government and private agencies, higher education institutions, and organizations that advocate on behalf of young children and their families.

- **A shared set of outcomes** for early childhood professional preparation. These core standards outline a set of common expectations for professional knowledge, skills and dispositions in six core areas. They express what tomorrow's early childhood professionals should know and be able to do.

- **A multidisciplinary approach** with an emphasis on assessment of outcomes and balanced attention to knowledge, skills, and dispositions.

Over time, NAEYC has organized these standards in a variety of ways. In the 1980s, they were organized into two position statements, one for associate degree programs and the other for four- and five-year degree programs. In 1991 one document outlined standards for basic and advanced degree programs. In 1999–2003, three documents outlined standards for associate, initial licensure, and advanced degree programs. In this new position statement, the core standards are presented in *one* NAEYC position statement that emphasizes the essentials of professional preparation for careers in early childhood education, regardless of role, setting, or degree level. This position statement will guide the preparation of supporting materials when these standards are adopted for use in the NCATE and ECADA accreditation systems.

Connecting to accreditation

Many higher education institutions choose to seek NAEYC Early Childhood Associate Degree Accreditation (ECADA) or NAEYC recognition of baccalaureate and graduate degrees as part of the National Council for Accreditation of Teacher Education (NCATE) accreditation for programs leading to initial or advanced teacher licensure. Both accreditation systems use these standards. Note that in these core NAEYC standards, the terms *students* and *candidates* are used interchangeably to describe the adults who are prepared by early childhood teacher education programs.

Note that these core standards are student performance standards. Meeting these standards requires evidence that programs (1) offer learning opportunities aligned with the key elements of the standards, (2) design key assessments that measure students' performance on key elements of the standards, (3) collect and aggregate data on student performance related to the standards, and (4) use that data in intentional, responsive ways to improve the quality of teaching and learning in the program.

These core standards are used across both ECADA and NCATE accreditation systems and across associate, baccalaureate, and graduate degree levels. Specific accreditation expectations related to different degree types and levels are published and updated separately for each accreditation system. Indicators of strength in program context and structure—the institutional mission, conceptual framework, field experiences, student characteristics and support services, faculty composition and qualifications, program resources and governance, support for transfer and articulation—are addressed in the guiding materials for programs seeking ECADA and NCATE accreditation.

Defining professional preparation in early childhood education

NAEYC continues to use the child development research and evidence base to define the "early childhood" period as spanning the years from birth through age 8. As in past editions of its standards, NAEYC recognizes that within that range, early childhood professionals—and the programs that prepare them—may choose to specialize within the early childhood spectrum (infants/toddlers, preschool/prekindergarten, or early primary grades).

Multiple professional roles and pathways

Specialization can be valuable, but NAEYC believes that all early childhood professionals should have a broad knowledge of development and learning across the birth-through-age-8 range; should be familiar with appropriate curriculum and assessment approaches across that age span; and should have in-depth knowledge and skills in at least two of the three periods: infants/toddlers, preschool/prekindergarten, and early primary grades. Without knowing about the *past* and the *future* (the precursors to children's current development and learning and the trajectory they will follow in later years), teachers cannot design effective learning opportunities within their specific professional assignment.

In addition, today's inclusive early childhood settings—those that include young children with developmental delays and disabilities—require knowledge of an even wider range of development and learning than was needed in many classrooms of the past. Without understanding a variety of professional settings and roles, as well as current and historical issues and trends that shape those settings and roles, individuals will find career and leadership opportunities in the field limited.

Many early childhood students enter college with a limited view of professional options. While all early childhood professionals should be well grounded in best practices in direct care and education, early childhood degree programs might also prepare students for work in the following roles and settings:

Early childhood educator roles, such as early childhood classroom teacher, family child care provider, Head Start teacher, or paraprofessional in the public schools;

Home-family support roles, such as home visitor, family advocate, child protective services worker, or parent educator; or

Professional support roles, such as early childhood administrator in a child care or Head Start program, staff trainer, peer/program mentor, or advocate at the community, state, or national level.

Core values in professional preparation

NAEYC's standards for professional preparation are derived from the developmental and educational research base found in the resources at the end of this document and in related position statements, including, among others,

- Developmentally Appropriate Practice in Early Childhood Programs Serving Children from Birth through Age 8;

- Early Learning Standards: Creating Conditions for Success;

- Early Childhood Mathematics: Promoting Good Beginnings;

- Learning to Read and Write: Developmentally Appropriate Practices for Young Children;

- Screening and Assessment of Young English-Language Learners;

- Promoting Positive Outcomes for Children with Disabilities: Recommendations for Curriculum, Assessment, and Program Evaluation;

- Responding to Linguistic and Cultural Diversity: Recommendations for Effective Early Childhood Education;

- Still Unacceptable Trends in Kindergarten Entry and Placement; and

- Early Childhood Curriculum, Assessment, and Program Evaluation. www.naeyc.org/positionstatements

In addition to the common research base and emphasis on the centrality of field experiences, these NAEYC standards affirm the value of, for example: play in children's lives; reciprocal relationships with families; child development knowledge as a foundation for professional practice; practices and curricula that are culturally respectful and responsive; ethical behavior and professional advocacy; and in-depth field experiences in high-quality professional preparation.

To be an excellent teacher: Professional preparation as meaning making

Young children benefit from well-planned, intentionally implemented, culturally relevant curriculum that both supports and challenges them. Research indicates the kinds of experiences that are essential to building later competence in such critical areas as language and literacy, mathematics, and other academic disciplines, as well as in gross motor development, social skills, emotional understanding, and self-regulation. The knowledge base also emphasizes the need for close relationships between young children and adults and between teachers and children's families. Such relationships and the secure base that they create are investments in children's later social, emotional, and academic competence.

Just as curriculum for young children is more than a list of skills to be mastered, professional preparation for early childhood teachers is more than a list of competencies to be assessed or a course list to complete. Early childhood students in well-designed programs develop professional knowledge, skills, and dispositions in a community of learners making sense of readings, observations, field experiences, and group projects through their interactions with others. They make connections between life experiences and new learning. They apply foundational concepts from general education course work to early childhood practice. They learn to self-assess and to advocate for themselves as students and as professionals. They strengthen their skills in written and verbal communication, learn to identify and use professional resources, and make connections between these "college skills" and lifelong professional practice.

Just as children learn best from teachers who use responsive and intentional strategies, adult students learn from instructors who create a caring community of learners, teach to enhance development and learning, plan curriculum aligned with important learning outcomes, assess student growth and development related to those outcomes, and build positive relationships with students and other stakeholders in the program.

Responding to current challenges, needs, and opportunities

Diversity, inclusion, and inequity

Every sector of the early childhood education community, including professional preparation programs, faces new challenges. Among them is the increased *diversity* of children and families in early childhood programs, from infant/toddler child care through the primary grades. This increased diversity is seen in the large numbers of children from culturally and linguistically diverse communities, as well as in the growing numbers of children with disabilities and other special learning needs who attend early childhood programs. A related challenge is the need to grow a more diverse teaching workforce and a more diverse leadership for the profession as a whole.

Another current challenge is the need to address the *inequities* and gaps in early learning that increase over time, developing into persistent achievement gaps in subgroups of American school children. Differences in academic achievement among ethnic groups, explained largely by socioeconomic differences, are central to the current "standards/accountability" movement in education—from infancy through the early primary grades and again as instructors of adults in early childhood preparation programs. To implement developmentally appropriate practices, early childhood professionals must "apply new knowledge to critical issues" facing the field (Copple & Bredekamp 2009).

One strategy to address these learning gaps and support children is the growth of publicly funded prekindergarten programs. Along with this strategy has come a new focus on preK-3 curriculum alignment; more high-quality professional development for teachers; partnerships between states, universities, community colleges, quality rating systems, and schools; and more highly qualified teachers in prekindergarten and early primary grades—teachers who have completed higher education degree programs with specialized early childhood preparation (Haynes 2009).

Preparation across the birth-through-8 age range

Professional preparation program leaders must make difficult decisions as they work with limited resources to design curriculum, field experiences, and assessment systems to prepare teachers for work across the full spectrum of the early childhood age range. Teacher licensure complicates the picture, since states' definitions of the early childhood age span and its subdivisions vary greatly and are changed frequently. Even programs that emphasize the upper end of the age range may not adequately prepare candidates in the critical content or subject matter areas needed to build children's academic success. Literacy is only one example: National reports (e.g., National Institute of Child Health and Human Development 2000) repeatedly fault teacher education for failing to provide candidates with research-based knowledge about reading and in-depth practical experience. An equally important concern is the tendency for teacher education programs to give inadequate attention to children's critical early years, especially the birth-to-age-3 period. Teachers who take positions in infant/toddler care but whose preparation has slighted that period may fail to support children's learning and development because the curriculum and teaching strategies they were taught to use are more effective with older children.

Programs also make difficult decisions related to *inclusion, diversity, and inequities* in adult education and in the early childhood field. Calls for greater formal education have not been matched by public investments in salaries and working conditions for early childhood staff, especially in early childhood programs in community-based settings that serve the vast majority of children under age 5.

Across all degree levels, NAEYC cautions programs against the superficial "mile wide and inch deep" model of professional preparation. Looking at the standards in this document, program faculty will be challenged to weigh breadth versus depth (standard by standard and element by element) within the context of their own program, student needs (including the need to acquire concepts and skills in general education), and the realities of a degree completion time frame. Every degree program that specializes in early childhood education has a responsibility to address all of the standards, each in its own way and with its own best decisions on breadth and depth. Like houses that start out with the same foundation and framework but look entirely different as rooms are added, combined, altered, and personalized, each professional preparation program may implement these standards in distinctive ways—as long as what is implemented is of uniformly high quality.

Field experiences

A key component of each of NAEYC's standards is hands-on field or clinical experiences, whether this is immersion in applied research for the doctoral student, systematic inquiry into their own classroom practices for the student already working in the field, or field observations for the student considering an early childhood career. Excellence in teaching requires a continuous interplay of theory, research, and practice. Supervised, reflective field experiences are critical to high-quality professional preparation. Rather than a separate standard on field experiences, programs should note that each standard includes a key element focused on application or use of knowledge and skills related to the standard. These key elements are best learned, practiced and assessed in field experiences.

The Professional Development School movement underscores the challenge of identifying and partnering with high-quality sites for education professionals to develop or refine their skills with competent mentorship and supervision. Finding a high-quality field site is a challenge across all early childhood settings—whether primary school, private preschool, child care center, or family child care home.

Many programs are working with states, communities, or local school districts to raise the qualifications of teachers already in the field—students who need to complete degree programs while maintaining current staff positions. These students may be already working in child care, Head Start, or as aides in primary grade classrooms. Other programs are deliberately providing field experiences in high-need/low-resource schools. In any of these cases, the quality of the site may not be high but the field placement may be selected for other reasons. The strongest indicator of quality is the quality of the student's opportunities to learn and practice, not the quality of the site itself.

Field experiences consistent with outcomes emphasized in NAEYC standards are

- **Well planned and sequenced,** and allow students to integrate theory, research, and practice.

- **Supported by faculty and other supervisors** who help students to make meaning of their experiences in early childhood settings and to evaluate those experiences against standards of quality.

- **Selected to expose students to a variety** of cultural, linguistic, and ethnic settings for early childhood care and education.

- **When the settings used for field experiences** do not reflect standards of quality, students are provided with other models and/or experiences to ensure that they are learning to work with young children and families in ways consistent with the NAEYC standards.

Faculty development

Strong professional preparation programs ensure that faculty members demonstrate the qualifications and characteristics needed to promote students' learning in relation to the NAEYC standards. Both full- and part-time faculty should have the academic and practical expertise to guide students toward mastery of the competencies reflected in NAEYC standards. In many programs, current faculty are aging and do not reflect the diversity of children or of adult college students served.

In 2008, NAEYC and the Society for Research in Child Development (SRCD) convened a meeting to develop recommendations that would advance the field of early childhood and improve outcomes for young children, especially those living in the most vulnerable circumstances. Final recommendations included,

> "Create and evaluate a sustainable system of faculty professional development that incorporates adult learning principles and evidence-based practices for improving outcomes for the most vulnerable children" and

> "Convene teacher preparation associations (e.g., the American Association of Colleges of Teacher Education [AACTE]) to brainstorm strategies that will increase the total number of future teacher educators, faculty, and researchers, especially from ethnically diverse backgrounds" (NAEYC & SRCD 2008, p. 593).

While strong programs put together a team of full- and part-time faculty members who each make an individual contribution, programs will be best prepared to meet the NAEYC standards when—

- All faculty are academically qualified for their specific professional roles; have had direct, substantial, professional experience; and continue to enhance their expertise in the early childhood profession.

- Faculty hold graduate degrees in early childhood education/child development or substantive early childhood course work at the graduate level and have demonstrated competence in each field of specialization they teach.

- Faculty know about and implement the principles in the position statements, NAEYC Code of Ethical Conduct and Statement of Commitment, in addition to its Supplement for Early Childhood Adult Educators.

- The program uses a variety of strategies to recruit, hire, mentor, and retain a diverse faculty.

The growing role of community colleges in teacher education

The early childhood field is increasingly committed to identifying and supporting a more diverse group of talented leaders. High-quality community college degree programs offer a promising route toward closing that gap. These programs play a critical role in providing access to higher education—and to the positions that require such education—for many groups, especially those currently underrepresented in professional leadership roles.

Cost, location, scheduling, or students' previous educational experiences can impede access to postsecondary education. Community colleges have the explicit mission of increasing access to higher education programs. Consequently, most community colleges offer courses in English as a second language and developmental courses in reading, writing, and mathematics for students who need that additional support.

Almost half of all higher education students in the United States—including 43 percent of African American and the majority of Native American and Hispanic undergraduates—are enrolled in community colleges. Two-thirds of community college students attend part-time. More than 80 percent of community college students work either full- or part-time, and 39 percent are the first in their families to attend college (AACC 2009).

As part of their effort to be responsive to students' varied needs, community colleges offer a variety of educational or degree options. The American Association of Community Colleges (AACC) recommends the following terminology: The Associate of Arts (A.A) degree generally emphasizes the arts, humanities, and social sciences; typically, three-quarters of the work required is general education course work. The Associate of Sciences (AS) degree generally requires one-half of the course work in general education, with substantial mathematics and science. The Associate in Applied Science (A.A.S) degree prepares the student for direct employment, with one third of the course work in general education. While many students who seek A.A.S degrees do not intend to transfer, these degrees are not intended to create barriers to transfer. "The [A.A.S] degree programs must be designed to recognize this dual possibility and to encourage students to recognize the long-term career possibilities that continued academic study will create" (AACC 1998).

According to estimates from Early and Winton's (2001) national sample, more than 700 institutions of higher education offer associate degree programs in early childhood education. The majority of these are in community colleges. The general community college population is more culturally and linguistically diverse than the student populations in other institutions of higher learning. Early childhood students in two-year programs represent greater diversity than do early childhood students in four-year programs.

Increasing numbers of students entering early childhood associate degree programs have been working—most in child care or Head Start programs (Early & Winton 2001). Many of those students continue to work while attending college part-time. These students are taking the lead in their own education, developing long-term career goals as they improve the quality of their current work with young children and families.

The career goals of students in these programs vary. For some, the degree may enhance their current position, build on a prior Child Development Associate (CDA) credential, and perhaps lead to greater responsibilities in the setting where they work. Although these work settings vary widely, Early and Winton's (2001) data suggest that proportionately more associate degree students work or plan to work with infants and toddlers than do students in four-year programs and many entering students have been working in family child care or child care administrative positions.

Transfer and articulation: meeting immediate needs while keeping doors open

Most early childhood associate degree programs focus on preparing students for direct work with young children in settings outside of primary school classrooms—positions that generally do not require baccalaureate degrees or early childhood teacher certification. However, many community college students are planning to transfer into a four-year college, heading toward teacher certification or other work in the early childhood field. A strong general education foundation together with an introduction to early childhood professional issues and skills is often the combination these students seek.

Still other students enter a community college program with a relatively limited set of objectives (e.g., to take one course that meets a child care licensing requirement or to receive college credit for work toward the CDA) but find unexpected pleasure and challenge in higher education. With support, such students often continue through the associate degree toward a baccalaureate degree and beyond.

Students who need time to succeed in developmental reading, writing, and mathematics courses also need time to develop confidence, skills, and career goals before deciding whether to seek transfer into a four-year institution. Early tracking of students into nontransfer or terminal programs can perpetuate the idea that little education is needed to teach our youngest children. In addition, premature tracking may create unnecessary barriers to students' future options—a serious concern given the higher proportions of students of color in community college programs. Tracking students into nontransfer programs deprives the field of opportunities for these students to become part of a more diverse leadership.

The strongest associate and baccalaureate degree programs serving students already in the field are attempting to keep transfer doors open through high-quality professional course work offered concurrently with strong general education and also by designing programs that simultaneously enhance one's current practice while still maintain transfer options from associate to baccalaureate to graduate degree programs. Increasing numbers of associate degree programs are offering distance learning, noncredit to credit course work, courses offered at worksites, and specialized courses that support particular settings and roles such as family child care or infant/toddler teacher.

Institutional and policy supports

Two recent surveys indicate some of the challenges facing early childhood degree programs as they strive to deliver high quality birth-through-age-8 preparation. A 2006 study found that only one-third (266) of accredited early childhood baccalaureate degree programs were designed as four-year programs, were housed in regionally accredited institutions of higher education, and offered both preschool and K–3 preparation. The study examines explicit and embedded preparation for diverse, multicultural, or inclusive classrooms and recommends a more comprehensive developmental theory and pedagogy, "transformation" of faculty, and attention to developing new leaders. The capacity of institutions and faculty to undertake these deep quality improvements is unclear, as are the market constraints posed by competition from alternative certification programs and from teacher specializations that are in more demand in the job market (Ray, Bowman, & Robbins 2006).

Hyson et al. (2009) surveyed 231 of an estimated 1,200 higher education institutions offering a degree in early childhood education. A large majority of programs at all degree levels (72 to 77 percent) relied heavily on NAEYC standards to guide program quality and improvement work. Most frequently, improvement efforts were focused on developing new student assessments, improving field experiences, and redesigning course work. Across degree levels, programs were focused on improvements related to preparation for linguistic and cultural diversity and to appropriate assessment of young children. The study makes a number of recommendations, including (1) invest in more full-time faculty with early childhood backgrounds, (2) expand faculty knowledge about research and evidence-based practices, (3) promote and support accreditation for higher education programs, and (4) strengthen connections between associate, baccalaureate, and graduate programs.

NAEYC's *Workforce Designs: A Public Policy Blueprint for State Early Childhood Professional Development Systems* offers guiding principles for states as they develop policy related to professional standards, career pathways, articulation, advisory structures, data, and financing. These guiding principles promote stronger integration across early childhood systems (teacher licensing, Head Start, prekindergarten, child care); quality improvement beyond minimum requirements; attention to diversity, inclusion and access issues; and building in compensation parity with rising qualifications (LeMoine 2008).

High-quality early childhood programs develop intentional responses to these current challenges. While a number of programs are engaged in quality improvements and innovative initiatives, there is a pressing need for faculty leadership from both current and new faculty as well as for institutional and policy support for efforts to improve early childhood professional preparation (e.g., Bowman 2000; Zaslow 2005; Washington 2008; Lutton 2009).

Components and organization of the standards

The standards that follow include a number of interconnected components. Those components, and their organization, are outlined below.

Core standards

There are six core standards, each of which describes in a few sentences what well-prepared students should know and be able to do. It is important to note, then, that the standard is not just that students know something about child development and learning—the expectations are more specific and complex than that.

Supporting explanations

Each standard includes a rationale or "supporting explanation," which offers a general description of why that standard is important.

Key elements

Three to five "key elements" within each standard clarify its most important features. These key elements break out components of each standard, highlighting what students should know, understand, and be able to do.

Examples of opportunities to learn and practice and of learning assessments

Guidance for programs seeking ECADA and NCATE accreditation will include examples of how early childhood degree programs might help students learn and practice the knowledge, skills, and professional dispositions within that aspect of the standard.

Accreditation materials will also include examples of opportunities to learn and practice—examples of ways that faculty might assess or document student growth and development.

Terminology

Assessment. In these standards the term *assessment* refers primarily to the methods through which early childhood professionals gain understanding of children's development and learning. Systematic observations and other informal and formal assessments enable candidates to appreciate children's unique qualities, to develop appropriate goals, and to plan, implement, and evaluate effective curriculum (see Standard 3). Secondarily, *assessment*, here, refers to the formal and informal assessments of adult students as required for degree completion. In higher education accreditation systems, these are referred to as "key assessments" and provide evidence that the degree program and its graduates meet the NAEYC standards.

Candidates/students. Refers to college students who are candidates for completion of an early childhood professional preparation program. In some cases, these students are also candidates for professional licensure or certification.

Children. This term is used throughout the standards rather than *students* to refer to the young children in early childhood classrooms, child care homes, and other early childhood settings. In this document, child/children refers to young children in the period of early childhood development, from birth through age 8.

Culture. Includes ethnicity, racial identity, economic class, family structure, language, and religious and political beliefs, which profoundly influence each child's development and relationship to the world.

Developmentally Appropriate Practice. Refers to the NAEYC position statement first developed in 1985 and most recently revised in 2009. The term *developmentally appropriate practice*, or DAP for short, refers to a framework of principles and guidelines for practice that promotes young children's optimal learning and development.

Field experiences. Includes field observations, fieldwork, practica, and student teaching or other clinical experiences such as home visiting.

Inclusion and diversity. Is not a separate standard, but is integrated into each standard. The phrase "each child" or "all children" is used to emphasize that every standard is meant to include all children: children with developmental delays or disabilities, children who are gifted and talented, children whose families are culturally and linguistically diverse, children from diverse socioeconomic groups, and other children with individual learning styles, strengths, and needs.

Technology. Is not a separate standard, but is woven throughout the standards. Early childhood teachers understand technology and media as important influences on children's development. They use technology as one way of communicating with families and sharing children's work, while recognizing the importance of using other communication methods for families with limited internet access. Similarly, they use technology in child assessment and as a professional resource with colleagues and for their own professional development.

Young children. Refers to children in the developmental period known as early childhood. Although developmental periods do not rigidly correspond to chronological age, early childhood is generally defined as including all children from birth through age 8.

Standards Summary

STANDARD 1. Promoting Child Development and Learning

Candidates prepared in early childhood degree programs are grounded in a child development knowledge base. They use their understanding of a) young children's characteristics and needs, and b) multiple interacting influences on children's development and learning, to c) create environments that are healthy, respectful, supportive, and challenging for each child.

STANDARD 2. Building Family and Community Relationships

Candidates prepared in early childhood degree programs understand that successful early childhood education depends upon partnerships with children's families and communities. They a) know about, understand, and value the importance and complex characteristics of children's families and communities. They use this understanding to b) create respectful, reciprocal relationships that support and empower families, and c) to involve all families in their children's development and learning.

STANDARD 3. Observing, Documenting, and Assessing to Support Young Children and Families

Candidates prepared in early childhood degree programs understand that child observation, documentation, and other forms of assessment are central to the practice of all early childhood professionals. They a) know about and understand the goals, benefits, and uses of assessment. They b) know about and use systematic observations, documentation, and other effective assessment strategies c) in a responsible way, d) in partnership with families and other professionals, to positively influence the development of every child.

STANDARD 4. Using Developmentally Effective Approaches

Candidates prepared in early childhood degree programs understand that teaching and learning with young children is a complex enterprise, and its details vary depending on children's ages, characteristics, and the settings within which teaching and learning occur. They a) understand and use positive relationships and supportive interactions as the foundation for their work with young children and families. Candidates b, c) know, understand, and use a wide array of developmentally appropriate approaches, instructional strategies, and tools to connect with children and families and d) positively influence each child's development and learning.

STANDARD 5. Using Content Knowledge to Build Meaningful Curriculum

Candidates prepared in early childhood degree programs a) use their knowledge of academic disciplines to design, implement, and evaluate experiences that promote positive development and learning for each and every young child. Candidates understand the importance of developmental domains and academic (or content) disciplines in early childhood curriculum. They b) know the essential concepts, inquiry tools, and structure of content areas, including academic subjects, and can identify resources to deepen their understanding. Candidates c) use their own knowledge and other resources to design, implement, and evaluate meaningful, challenging curriculum that promotes comprehensive developmental and learning outcomes for every young child.

STANDARD 6. Becoming a Professional

Candidates prepared in early childhood degree programs a) identify and conduct themselves as members of the early childhood profession. They b) know and use ethical guidelines and other professional standards related to early childhood practice. They c) are continuous, collaborative learners who demonstrate knowledgeable, reflective and critical perspectives on their work, making informed decisions that d) integrate knowledge from a variety of sources. They are e) informed advocates for sound educational practices and policies.

Standard 1
Promoting Child Development and Learning

Students prepared in early childhood degree programs are grounded in a child development knowledge base. They use their understanding of young children's characteristics and needs and of the multiple interacting influences on children's development and learning to create environments that are healthy, respectful, supportive, and challenging for each child.

Key elements of Standard 1

1a: Knowing and understanding young children's characteristics and needs

1b: Knowing and understanding the multiple influences on development and learning

1c: Using developmental knowledge to create healthy, respectful, supportive, and challenging learning environments

Supporting explanation

The early childhood field has historically been grounded in a child development knowledge base, and early childhood programs have aimed to support a broad range of positive developmental outcomes for all young children. Although the scope and emphasis of that knowledge base have changed over the years and while early childhood professionals recognize that other sources of knowledge are also important influences on curriculum and programs for young children, early childhood practice continues to be deeply linked with a "sympathetic understanding of the young child" (Elkind 1994).

Well-prepared early childhood degree candidates base their practice on sound **knowledge and understanding of young children's characteristics and needs.** This foundation encompasses multiple, interrelated areas of children's development and learning—including physical, cognitive, social, emotional, language, and aesthetic domains; play, activity, and learning processes; and motivation to learn—and is supported by coherent theoretical perspectives and by current research.

Candidates also understand and apply their understanding of the **multiple influences on young children's development and learning** and

of how those influences may interact to affect development in both positive and negative ways. Those influences include the cultural and linguistic contexts for development, children's close relationships with adults and peers, economic conditions of children and families, children's health status and disabilities individual developmental variations and learning styles, opportunities to play and learn, technology and the media, and family and community characteristics. Candidates also understand the potential influence of early childhood programs, including early intervention, on short- and long-term outcomes for children.

Candidates' competence is demonstrated in their ability to **use developmental knowledge to create healthy, respectful, supportive, and challenging learning environments** for all young children (including curriculum, interactions, teaching practices, and learning materials). Such environments reflect *four critical features*.

- First, the environments are *healthy*—that is, candidates possess the knowledge and skills needed to promote young children's physical and psychological health, safety, and sense of security.

- Second, the environments reflect *respect* for each child as a feeling, thinking individual and then for each child's culture, home language, individual abilities or disabilities, family context, and community. In respectful environments, candidates model and affirm antibias perspectives on development and learning.

- Third, the learning environments created by early childhood teacher candidates are supportive. Candidates demonstrate their belief in young children's ability to learn, and they show that they can use their understanding of early childhood development to help each child understand and make meaning from her or his experiences through play, spontaneous activity, and guided investigations.

- Finally, the learning environments that early childhood candidates create are appropriately *challenging*. In other words, candidates apply their knowledge of contemporary theory and research to construct learning environments that provide achievable and stretching experiences for all children—including children with special abilities and children with disabilities or developmental delays.

Standard 2
Building Family and Community Relationships

Students prepared in early childhood degree programs understand that successful early childhood education depends upon partnerships with children's families and communities. They know about, understand, and value the importance and complex characteristics of children's families and communities. They use this understanding to create respectful, reciprocal relationships that support and empower families and to involve all families in their children's development and learning.

Key elements of Standard 2

2a: Knowing about and understanding diverse family and community characteristics

2b: Supporting and engaging families and communities through respectful, reciprocal relationships

2c: Involving families and communities in their children's development and learning

Supporting explanation

Because young children's lives are so embedded in their families and communities and research indicates that successful early childhood education depends upon partnerships with families and communities, early childhood professionals need to thoroughly understand and apply their knowledge in this area.

First, well-prepared candidates possess **knowledge and understanding of diverse family and community characteristics** and of the many influences on families and communities. Family theory and research provide a knowledge base. Socioeconomic conditions; family structures, relationships, stresses, and supports (including the impact of having a child with special needs); home language; cultural values; ethnicity; community resources, cohesiveness, and organization—knowledge of these and other factors creates a deeper understanding of young children's lives. This knowledge is critical to the candidates' ability to help children learn and develop well.

Second, candidates possess the knowledge and skills needed to **support and engage diverse families through respectful, reciprocal relationships.** Candidates understand how to build positive relationships, taking families' preferences and goals into account and incorporating knowledge of families' languages and cultures. Candidates demonstrate respect for variations across cultures in family strengths, expectations, values, and childrearing practices. Candidates consider family members to be resources for insight into their children, as well as resources for curriculum and program development. Candidates know about and demonstrate a variety of communication skills to foster such relationships, emphasizing informal conversations while also including appropriate uses of conferencing and technology to share children's work and to communicate with families.

In their work, early childhood teacher candidates develop cultural competence as they build relationships with diverse families, including those whose children have disabilities or special characteristics or learning needs; families who are facing multiple challenges in their lives; and families whose languages and cultures may differ from those of the early childhood professional. Candidates also understand that their relationships with families include assisting families in finding needed resources, such as mental health services, health care, adult education, English language instruction, and economic assistance that may contribute directly or indirectly to their children's positive development and learning. Well-prepared early childhood candidates are able to identify such resources and know how to connect families with appropriate services, including help with planning transitions from one educational or service system to another.

Finally, well-prepared candidates possess essential skills to **involve families and communities in many aspects of children's development and learning.** They understand and value the role of parents and other important family members as children's primary teachers. Candidates understand how to go beyond parent conferences to engage families in curriculum planning, assessing children's learning, and planning for children's transitions to new programs. When their approaches to family involvement are not effective, candidates evaluate and modify those approaches rather than assuming that families "are just not interested."

Standard 3
Observing, Documenting, and Assessing to Support Young Children and Families

Students prepared in early childhood degree programs understand that child observation, documentation, and other forms of assessment are central to the practice of all early childhood professionals. They know about and understand the goals, benefits, and uses of assessment. They know about and use systematic observations, documentation, and other effective assessment strategies in a responsible way, in partnership with families and other professionals, to positively influence the development of every child.

Key elements of Standard 3

3a: Understanding the goals, benefits, and uses of assessment

3b: Knowing about and using observation, documentation, and other appropriate assessment tools and approaches

3c: Understanding and practicing responsible assessment to promote positive outcomes for each child

3d: Knowing about assessment partnerships with families and with professional colleagues

Supporting explanation

Although definitions vary, in these standards the term *assessment* includes all methods through which early childhood professionals gain understanding of children's development and learning. Ongoing, systematic observations and other informal and formal assessments are essential for candidates to appreciate children's unique qualities, to develop appropriate goals, and to plan, implement, and evaluate effective curriculum. Although assessment may take many forms, early childhood candidates demonstrate its central role by embedding assessment-related activities in curriculum and daily routines so that assessment becomes a habitual part of professional life.

Well-prepared early childhood candidates can explain the central **goals, benefits, and uses of assessment.** In considering the goals of assessment, candidates articulate and apply the concept of *alignment*—good assessment is consistent with and connected to appropriate goals, curriculum,

and teaching strategies for young children. The candidates know how to use assessment as a positive tool that supports children's development and learning and improves outcomes for young children and families. Candidates are able to explain positive uses of assessment and exemplify these in their own work, while also showing an awareness of the potentially negative uses of assessment in early childhood programs and policies.

Many aspects of effective assessment require collaboration with families and with other professionals. Through **partnerships with families and with professional colleagues**, candidates use positive assessment to identify the strengths of families and children. Through appropriate screening and referral, assessment may also result in identifying children who may benefit from special services. Both family members and, as appropriate, members of interprofessional teams may be involved in assessing children's development, strengths, and needs. As new practitioners, candidates may have had limited opportunities to experience such partnerships, but they demonstrate essential knowledge and core skills in team building and in communicating with families and colleagues from other disciplines.

Early childhood assessment includes **observation and documentation and other appropriate assessment strategies.** Effective teaching of young children begins with thoughtful, appreciative, systematic observation and documentation of each child's unique qualities, strengths, and needs. Observation gives insight into how young children develop and how they respond to opportunities and obstacles in their lives. Observing young children in classrooms, homes, and communities helps candidates develop a broad sense of who children are—as individuals, as group members, as family members, as members of cultural and linguistic communities. Candidates demonstrate skills in conducting systematic observations, interpreting those observations, and reflecting on their significance. Because spontaneous *play* is such a powerful window on all aspects of children's development, well-prepared candidates create opportunities to observe children in playful situations as well as in more formal learning contexts.

Many *young children with disabilities* are included in early childhood programs, and early identification of children with developmental delays or disabilities is very important. All beginning professionals, therefore, need essential knowledge about how to collect relevant information, including appropriate uses of screening tools and play-based assessments, not only for their own planning but also to share with families and with other professionals. Well-prepared candidates are able to choose valid tools that are developmentally, culturally, and linguistically appropriate; use the tools correctly; adapt tools as needed, using assistive technology as a resource; make appropriate referrals; and interpret assessment results, with the goal of obtaining valid, useful information to inform practice and decision making.

Although assessment can be a positive tool for early childhood professionals, it has also been used in inappropriate and harmful ways. Well-prepared candidates understand and practice **responsible assessment.** Candidates understand that responsible assessment is ethically grounded and guided by sound professional standards. It is collaborative and open. Responsible assessment supports children, rather than being used to exclude them or deny them services. Candidates demonstrate understanding of appropriate, responsible assessment practices for culturally and linguistically diverse children and for children with developmental delays, disabilities, or other special characteristics. Finally, candidates demonstrate knowledge of legal and ethical issues, current educational concerns and controversies, and appropriate practices in the assessment of diverse young children.

Standard 4
Using Developmentally Effective Approaches to Connect with Children and Families

Students prepared in early childhood degree programs understand that teaching and learning with young children is a complex enterprise, and its details vary depending on children's ages, characteristics, and the settings within which teaching and learning occur. They understand and use positive relationships and supportive interactions as the foundation for their work with young children and families. Students know, understand, and use a wide array of developmentally appropriate approaches, instructional strategies, and tools to connect with children and families and positively influence each child's development and learning.

Key elements of Standard 4

4a: Understanding positive relationships and supportive interactions as the foundation of their work with children

4b: Knowing and understanding effective strategies and tools for early education

4c: Using a broad repertoire of developmentally appropriate teaching/learning approaches

4d: Reflecting on their own practice to promote positive outcomes for each child

Supporting explanation

Early childhood candidates demonstrate that they understand the theories and research that support **the importance of relationships and high-quality interactions in early education**. In their practice, they display warm, nurturing interactions with each child, communicating genuine liking for and interest in young children's activities and characteristics. Throughout the years that children spend in early childhood settings, their successful learning is dependent not just on instruction but also on personal connections with important adults. Through these connections children develop not only academic skills but also positive learning dispositions and confidence in themselves as learners. Responsive teaching creates the conditions within which very young children can explore and learn about their world. The close attachments children develop with their teachers/caregivers, the expectations and beliefs that adults have about young children's capacities, and the warmth and responsiveness of adult-child interactions are powerful influences on positive developmental and educational outcomes. How children expect to be treated and how they treat others are significantly shaped in the early childhood setting. Candidates in early childhood programs develop the capacity to build a caring community of learners in the early childhood setting.

Early childhood professionals need **a broad repertoire of effective strategies and tools** to help young children learn and develop well. Candidates must ground their curriculum in a set of core approaches to teaching that are supported by research and are closely linked to the processes of early development and learning. In a sense, those approaches *are* the curriculum for infants and toddlers, although academic content can certainly be embedded in each of them. With preschool and early primary grade children, the relative weight and explicitness of subject matter or academic content become more evident in the curriculum, yet the core approaches or strategies remain as a consistent framework. Engaging conversations, thought-provoking questions, provision of materials, and spontaneous activities are all evident in the candidate's repertoire of teaching skills.

Candidates demonstrate the essential *dispositions* to develop positive, respectful relationships with children whose cultures and languages may differ from their own, as well as with children who may have developmental delays, disabilities, or other learning challenges. In making the transition from family to a group context, very young children need continuity between the practices of family members and those used by professionals in the early childhood setting. Their feelings of safety and confidence depend on that continuity. Candidates know the cultural practices and contexts of the young children they teach, and they adapt practices as they continue to develop *cultural competence*—culturally relevant knowledge and skills.

Well-prepared early childhood professionals make purposeful use of various learning formats based on their understanding of children as individuals and as part of a group, and on alignment with important educational and developmental goals. A flexible, research-based **repertoire of teaching/learning approaches to promote young children's development** includes

- Fostering oral language and communication

- Drawing from a continuum of teaching strategies

- Making the most of the environment, schedule, and routines

- Setting up all aspects of the indoor and outdoor environment

- Focusing on children's individual characteristics, needs, and interests

- Linking children's language and culture to the early childhood program

- Teaching through social interactions

- Creating support for play

- Addressing children's challenging behaviors

- Supporting learning through technology

- Using integrative approaches to curriculum

All of these teaching approaches are effective across the early childhood age span. From the infant/toddler room to the early grades, young children are developing not only early language and reading skills but also the *desire* to communicate, read, and write. They are developing not only early math and science skills and concepts but also the *motivation* to solve problems. They are developing empathy, sociability, friendships, self-concept and self-esteem. Concept acquisition, reasoning, self-regulation, planning and organization, emotional understanding and empathy, sociability—development of all of these is deeply entwined with early experiences in mathematics, language, literacy, science, and social studies in the early education program.

Early childhood professionals make decisions about their practice based on expertise. They make professional judgments through each day based on knowledge of child development and learning, individual children, and the social and cultural contexts in which children live. From this knowledge base, effective teachers design activities, routines, interactions and curriculum for specific children and groups of children. They consider both what to teach and how to teach, developing the habit of **reflective, responsive and intentional practice** to promote positive outcomes for each child.

Standard 5
Using Content Knowledge to Build Meaningful Curriculum

Students prepared in early childhood degree programs use their knowledge of academic disciplines to design, implement, and evaluate experiences that promote positive development and learning for each and every young child. Students understand the importance of developmental domains and academic (or content) disciplines in an early childhood curriculum. They know the essential concepts, inquiry tools, and structure of content areas, including academic subjects, and can identify resources to deepen their understanding. Students use their own knowledge and other resources to design, implement, and evaluate meaningful, challenging curricula that promote comprehensive developmental and learning outcomes for every young child.

Key elements of Standard 5

5a: Understanding content knowledge and resources in academic disciplines

5b: Knowing and using the central concepts, inquiry tools, and structures of content areas or academic disciplines

5c: Using their own knowledge, appropriate early learning standards, and other resources to design, implement, and evaluate meaningful, challenging curricula for each child.

Supporting explanation

Strong, effective early childhood curricula do not come out of a box or a teacher-proof manual. Early childhood professionals have an especially challenging task in developing effective curricula. As suggested in Standard 1, well-prepared candidates ground their practice in a thorough, research-based understanding of young children's development and learning processes. In developing curriculum, they recognize that every child constructs knowledge in personally and culturally familiar ways. In addition, in order to make curriculum powerful and accessible to all, well-prepared candidates develop curriculum that is free of biases related to ethnicity, religion, gender, or ability status—and, in fact, the curriculum actively counters such biases.

The teacher of children from birth through age 8 must be well versed in **the essential content knowledge and resources in many academic disciplines.** Because children are encountering those content areas for the first time, early childhood professionals set the foundations for later understanding and success. Going beyond conveying isolated facts, well-prepared early childhood candidates possess the kind of content knowledge that focuses on the "big ideas," methods of investigation and expression, and organization of the major academic disciplines. Thus, the early childhood professional knows not only *what* is important in each content area but also *why* it is important—how it links with earlier and later understandings both within and across areas. Because of its central place in later academic competence, the domain of language and literacy requires in-depth, research-based understanding and skill. Mathematics too is increasingly recognized as an essential foundation.

Teachers of young children demonstrate the understanding of **central concepts, inquiry tools, and structure of content areas** needed to provide appropriate environments that support learning in each content area for all children, beginning in infancy (through foundational developmental experiences) and extending through the primary grades. Candidates demonstrate basic knowledge of the research base underlying each content area and of the core concepts and standards of professional organizations in each content area. They rely on sound resources for that knowledge. Finally, candidates demonstrate that they can analyze and critique early childhood curriculum experiences in terms of the relationship of the experiences to the research base and to professional standards.

Well-prepared candidates choose their approaches to the task depending on the ages and developmental levels of the children they teach. They use their own **knowledge, appropriate early learning standards, and other resources to design, implement, and evaluate meaningful, challenging curriculum for each child.** With the youngest children, early childhood candidates emphasize the key experiences that will support later academic skills and understandings—with reliance on the core approaches and strategies described in Standard 4 and with emphasis on oral language and the development of children's background knowledge. Working with somewhat older or more skilled children, candidates also identify those aspects of each subject area that are critical to children's later academic competence. With all children, early childhood professionals support later success by modeling engagement in challenging subject matter and by building children's faith in themselves as young learners—young mathematicians, scientists, artists, readers, writers, historians, economists, and geographers (although children may not think of themselves in such categories).

Early Childhood curriculum content/discipline areas include learning goals, experiences, and assessment in the following academic disciplines or content areas:

- Language and literacy
- The arts—music, creative movement, dance, drama, and visual arts
- Mathematics
- Science
- Physical activity, physical education, health and safety
- Social studies

Designing, implementing, and evaluating meaningful, challenging curriculum requires alignment with appropriate early learning standards and knowledgeable use of the discipline's resources to focus on key experiences for each age group and each individual child.

Early childhood teacher candidates, just like experienced teachers, go beyond their own basic knowledge to identify and use high-quality resources, including books, standards documents, Web resources, and individuals who have specialized content expertise in developing early childhood curriculum. In addition to national or state standards (NAEYC & NAECS/SDE 2002), or several larger goals are also held by all early childhood teachers:

- **Security and self-regulation.** Appropriate, effective curriculum creates a secure base from which young children can explore and tackle challenging problems. Well-implemented curriculum also helps children become better able to manage or regulate their expressions of emotion and, over time, to cope with frustration and manage impulses effectively rather than creating high levels of frustration and anxiety.

- **Problem-solving and thinking skills.** Candidates who have skills in developing and implementing meaningful, challenging curricula will also support young children's ability—and motivation—to solve problems and think well.

- **Academic and social competence.** Because good early childhood curriculum is aligned with young children's developmental and learning styles, it supports the growth of academic and social skills.

With these goals in mind, candidates develop curriculum to include both planned and spontaneous experiences that are developmentally appropriate, meaningful, and challenging for all young children, including those with developmental delays or disabilities; address cultural and linguistic diversities; lead to positive learning outcomes; and, as children become older, develop positive dispositions toward learning within each content area.

Standard 6
Becoming a Professional

Students prepared in early childhood degree programs identify and conduct themselves as members of the early childhood profession. They know and use ethical guidelines and other professional standards related to early childhood practice. They are continuous, collaborative learners who demonstrate knowledgeable, reflective, and critical perspectives on their work, making informed decisions that integrate knowledge from a variety of sources. They are informed advocates for sound educational practices and policies.

Key elements of Standard 6

6a: Identifying and involving oneself with the early childhood field

6b: Knowing about and upholding ethical standards and other professional guidelines

6c: Engaging in continuous, collaborative learning to inform practice

6d: Integrating knowledgeable, reflective, and critical perspectives on early education

6e: Engaging in informed advocacy for children and the profession

The early childhood field has a distinctive history, values, knowledge base, and mission. Early childhood professionals, including beginning teachers, have a strong **identification and involvement with the early childhood field** to better serve young children and their families. Well-prepared candidates understand the nature of a profession. They know about the many connections between the early childhood field and other related disciplines and professions with which they may collaborate while serving diverse young children and families. Candidates are also aware of the broader contexts and challenges within which early childhood professionals work. They consider current issues and trends that might affect their work in the future.

Because young children are at such a critical point in their development and learning, and because they are vulnerable and cannot articulate their own rights and needs, early childhood professionals have compelling responsibilities to **know about and uphold ethical guidelines and other professional standards.** The profession's code of ethical conduct guides the practice of responsible early childhood educators. Well-prepared candidates are very familiar with NAEYC's Code of Ethical Conduct and are guided by its ideals and principles. This means honoring their responsibilities to uphold high standards of confidentiality, sensitivity, and respect for children, families, and colleagues. Candidates know how to use the Code to analyze and resolve professional ethical dilemmas and are able to give defensible justifications for their resolutions of those dilemmas. Well-prepared candidates also know and obey relevant laws, such as those pertaining to child abuse, the rights of children with disabilities, and school attendance. Finally, candidates are familiar with relevant professional guidelines, such as national, state, or local standards for content and child outcomes; position statements about, for example, early learning standards, linguistic and cultural diversity, early childhood mathematics, technology in early childhood, prevention of child abuse, child care licensing requirements, and other professional standards affecting early childhood practice.

Continuous, collaborative learning to inform practice is a hallmark of a professional in any field. An attitude of inquiry is evident in well-prepared candidates' writing, discussion, and actions. Whether engaging in classroom-based research, investigating ways to improve their own practices, participating in conferences, or finding resources in libraries and on Internet sites, candidates demonstrate self-motivated, purposeful learning that directly influences the quality of their work with young children. Candidates—and professional preparation programs—view graduation or licensure not as the final demonstration of competence but as one milestone among many, including professional development experiences before and beyond successful degree completion.

At its most powerful, learning is socially constructed in interaction with others. Even as beginning teachers, early childhood candidates demonstrate involvement in collaborative learning communities with other candidates, higher education faculty, and experienced early childhood practitioners. By working together on common challenges, with lively exchanges of ideas, members of such communities benefit from one another's perspectives. Candidates also demonstrate understanding of and essential skills in interdisciplinary collaboration. Because many children with disabilities and other special needs are included in early childhood programs, every practitioner needs to understand the role of the other professionals who may be involved in young children's care and education (e.g., special educators, reading specialists, speech and hearing specialists, physical and occupational therapists, school psychologists). Candidates demonstrate that they have the essential communication skills and knowledge base to engage in interdisciplinary team meetings as informed partners and to fulfill their roles as part of Individualized Family Service Plan and Individualized Education Program (IFSP/IEP) teams for children with developmental delays or disabilities. They use technology effectively with children, with peers, and as a professional resource.

Well-prepared candidates' practice is influenced by **knowledgeable, reflective, and critical perspectives.** As professionals, early childhood candidates' decisions and advocacy efforts are grounded in multiple sources of knowledge and multiple perspectives. Even routine decisions about what materials to use for an activity, whether to intervene in a dispute between two children, how to organize nap time, what to say about curriculum in a newsletter, or what to tell families about new video games are informed by a professional context, research-based knowledge, and values. In their work with young children, candidates show that they make and justify decisions on the basis of their *knowledge* of the central issues, professional values and standards, and research findings in their field. They also show evidence of *reflective approaches* to their work, analyzing their own practices in a broader context, and using reflections to modify and improve their work with young children. Finally, well-prepared candidates display a *critical stance*, examining their own work, sources of professional knowledge, and the early childhood field with a questioning attitude. Their work demonstrates that they do not just accept a simplistic source of truth; instead, they recognize that while early childhood educators share the same core professional values, they do not agree on all of the field's central questions. Candidates demonstrate an understanding that through dialogue and attention to differences, early childhood professionals will continue to reach new levels of shared knowledge.

Finally, early childhood candidates demonstrate that they can engage in **informed advocacy for children and families and the profession.**

They know about the central policy issues in the field, including professional compensation, financing of the early education system, and standards setting and assessment. They are aware of and engaged in examining ethical issues and societal concerns about program quality and provision of early childhood services and the implications of those issues for advocacy and policy change. Candidates have a basic understanding of how public policies are developed, and they demonstrate essential advocacy skills, including verbal and written communication and collaboration with others around common issues.

References

Introduction

AACC (American Association of Community Colleges). 2009a. AACC statement regarding the Project on Student Loan Debt report on community college loan access. www.aacc.nche.edu/About/Positions/Pages/ps04162008.aspx

AACC. 2009b. Fast facts. www.aacc.nche.edu/AboutCC/Pages/fastfacts.aspx

AACC. 1998. AACC position statement on the associate degree. www.aacc.nche.edu/About/Positions/Pages/ps08011998.aspx

Bogard, K., F. Traylor, & R. Takanishi. 2008. Teacher education and PK outcomes: Are we asking the right questions? *Early Childhood Research Quarterly* 23 (1): 1–6.

Burchinal, M., M. Hyson, & M. Zaslow. 2008. *Competencies and credentials for early childhood educators: What do we know and what do we need to know?* NHSA Dialog Briefs 11 (1).

Curenton, S. 2005. Toward better definition and measurement of early childhood professional development. In *Critical issues in early childhood professional development*, eds. M. Zaslow & I. Martinez-Beck, 17–19. Baltimore: Brookes.

Darling-Hammond, L. 2007. We need to invest in math and science teachers. *The Chronicle Review* 54 (17): B20. http://chronicle.com/weekly/v54/i17/17b02001.htm

Early, D., & P. Winton. 2001. Preparing the workforce: early childhood teacher preparation at 2- and 4-year institutions of higher education. *Early Childhood Research Quarterly* 16 (3): 285–306.

Gilliam, W. S. 2008. *Implementing policies to reduce the likelihood of preschool expulsion.* Foundation for Child Development FCD Policy Brief 7. http://medicine.yale.edu/childstudy/zigler/publications/34772_PreKExpulsionBrief2.pdf

Haynes, M., & J. Levin. 2009. *Promoting quality in preK-grade 3 classrooms: findings and results from NASBE's Early Childhood Education Network.* NASBE Issues in Brief. Arlington, VA: National Association of State Boards of Education.

Hyson, M., H.B. Tomlinson, & C.A.S. Morris. 2009. Quality improvement in early childhood teacher education faculty perspectives and recommendations for the future. *Early Childhood Research and Practice* 11 (1). http://ecrp.uiuc.edu/v11n1/hyson.html

Karp, N. 2005. Designing models for professional development at the local, state, and national levels. In *Critical issues in early childhood professional development*, eds. M. Zaslow & I. Martinez-Beck, 225–30. Baltimore: Brookes.

Kelly, P., & G. Camilli. 2007. *The impact of teacher education on outcomes in center-based early childhood education programs: A meta-analysis.* New Brunswick, NJ: National Institute for Early Education Research.

LeMoine, S. 2008 *Workforce designs: A policy blueprint for state early childhood professional development systems.* Washington, DC: NAEYC.

Lima, C., K.L. Maxwell, H. Able-Booneb, & C.R. Zimmer. 2009. Cultural and linguistic diversity in early childhood teacher preparation: The impact of contextual characteristics on coursework and practica. *Early Childhood Research Quarterly* 24 (1): 64–76.

Lutton, A.. 2009. NAEYC early childhood professional preparation standards: A vision for tomorrow's early childhood teachers. 2009. In *Conversations on early childhood teacher education: Voices from the Working Forum for Teacher Educators*, eds. A. Gibbons & C. Gibbs. Redmond, WA: World Forum Foundation and New Zealand Tertiary College.

Martinez-Beck, I., & M. Zaslow. 2005. Introduction: The context for critical issues in early childhood professional development. In *Critical issues in early childhood professional development*, eds. M. Zaslow & I. Martinez-Beck, 1-15. Baltimore: Brookes.

NAEYC & SRCD (Society for Research in Child Development). 2008. Using research to improve outcomes for young children: A call for action. Final report of the Wingspread Conference, September 18–20, 2007. *Early Childhood Research Quarterly* 23 (4): 591–96.

Ray, A.., B. Bowman, & J. Robbins. 2006. *Preparing early childhood teachers to successfully educate* all *children: The contribution of four-year undergraduate teacher preparation programs.* Report to the Foundation for Child Development on the Project on Race, Class, and Culture in Early Childhood. Chicago: Erikson Institute. www.erikson.edu/PageContent/en-us/Documents/pubs/Teachered.pdf

Snow, K.L. 2005. Completing the model: Connecting early child care worker professional development with child outcomes. In *Critical issues in early childhood professional development*, eds. M. Zaslow & I. Martinez-Beck, 137–140). Baltimore: Brookes.

Snyder, T.D., S.A. Dillow, & C.M. Hoffman. 2009. *Digest of education statistics 2008.* NCES #2009-020. Washington, DC: National Center for Education Statistics, Institute of Educational Sciences, U.S. Department of Education. http://nces.ed.gov/pubsearch/pubsinfo.asp?pubid=2009020

Tout, K., M. Zaslow, & D. Berry. 2005. Quality and qualifications: Links between professional development and quality in early care and education settings. In *Critical issues in early childhood professional development*, eds. M. Zaslow & I. Martinez-Beck, 77–110. Baltimore: Brookes.

Washington, V. 2008. *Role, relevance, reinvention: Higher education in the field of early care and education.* Boston: Wheelock College.

Whitebook, M., L. Sakai, F. Kipnis, M. Almaraz, F. Suarez, & D. Bellm. 2008. Learning together: A study of six B.A. completion cohort programs in early care and education. Year I Report. http://www.irle.berkeley.edu/cscce/wp-content/uploads/2008/07/learning_together08.pdf

Zaslow, M. 2005. Charting a course for improved professional development across varying programs and practices. In *Critical issues in early childhood professional development*, eds. M. Zaslow & I. Martinez-Beck, 351–53. Baltimore: Brookes.

Standard 1: Importance of Knowing Child Development

Bowman, B.T., S. Donovan, & M.S. Burns. 2000. *Eager to learn: Educating our preschoolers.* Washington, DC: National Academies Press. [1, 4]

Bronfenbrenner, U. 2004. *Making human beings human: Bioecological perspectives on human development.* Thousand Oaks, CA: Sage. [1]

Buysse, V., & P.W. Wesley. 2006. *Evidence-based practice in the early childhood field.* Washington, DC: Zero to Three Press. [1]

Copple, C., & S. Bredekamp, eds. 2009. *Developmentally appropriate practice in early childhood programs serving children from birth through age 8.* Washington, DC: NAEYC. [1, 4, 5]

Essa, E.L., M.M. & Burnham, eds.2009. *Informing our practice: Useful research on young children's development.* Washington, DC: NAEYC. [1,4]

Hendrick, J., & P. Weissman. 2009. *The whole child: Developmental education for the early years.* Upper Saddle River, NJ: Prentice Hall. [1]

National Research Council & Institute of Medicine. 2000 *From neurons to neighborhoods: The science of early childhood development.* Jack P. Shonkoff and Deborah A. Phillips, eds.; Committee on Integrating the Science of Early Childhood Development; Board on Children, Youth, and Families of the Commission on Behavioral and Social Sciences and Education. Washington, DC: National Academies Press. [1]

NCATE & NICHD (National Institute of Child Health and Human Development). 2006. *Child and adolescent development research and teacher education: Evidence-based pedagogy, policy, and practice.* Retrieved June 1, 2009 at http://www.ncate.org/dotnetnuke/LinkClick.aspx?fileticket=IKL54rTMZp8%3d&tabid=358 [1]

NICHD Early Child Care Research Network. 2005. *Child care and child development: Results from the NICHD Study of Early Child Care and Youth Development.* New York: Guilford. [1]

Rogoff, B. 2003. *The cultural nature of human development.* Oxford, UK: Oxford University Press. [1]

Tabors, P.O. 2008. One child, two languages: A guide for early childhood educators of children learning English as a second language. Baltimore, MD: Brookes. [1, 4]

Standard 2: Building Family and Community Relationships

Bouffard, S., & H. Weiss. 2008. Thinking big: A new framework for family involvement policy, practice, and research. *The Evaluation Exchange* 14 (1&2): 2–5. [2]

DEC (Division for Early Childhood) & NAEYC. 2008. Early childhood inclusion: Joint position statement of the Division for Early Childhood (DEC) and the National Association for the Education of Young Children (NAEYC). http://www.naeyc.org/files/naeyc/file/positions/DEC_NAEYC_EC_updatedKS.pdf [2]

Epstein, J. 2001. *School, family, and community partnerships: Preparing educators and improving schools.* Boulder, CO: Westview. [2]

Epstein, J. L., & S.B. Sheldon. 2006. *Moving forward: Ideas for research on school, family, and community partnerships.* Retrieved June 1, 2009 at www.csos.jhu.edu/P2000/pdf/Literature%20Review%20-%20Epstein%20and%20Sheldon%2006.pdf [2]

Henderson, A.T., & K.L. Mapp. 2002. *A new wave of evidence: The impact of school, family, and community connections on student achievement.* Austin, TX: National Center for Family & Community Connections with Schools, Southwest Educational Development Laboratory. Retrieved June 1, 2009 at www.sedl.org/connections/resources/evidence.pdf [2]

Lopez, M.E., H. Kreider, & M. Caspe. 2004. Co-constructing family involvement. *Evaluation Exchange* X (4): 2–3. [2]

Lynch, E.W., & M.J. Hanson. 2004. *Developing cross-cultural competence: A guide for working with children and their families.* Baltimore, MD: Brookes. [2]

Ray, A., B. Bowman, & J. Robbins. 2006. *Preparing early childhood teachers to successfully educate* all *children: The contribution of four-year undergraduate teacher preparation programs.* Report to the Foundation for Child Development on the Project on Race, Class, and Culture in Early Childhood. Chicago: Erikson Institute. www.erikson.edu/PageContent/en-us/Documents/pubs/Teachered.pdf

Valdés, G. 1999. *Con respeto: Bridging the distances between culturally diverse families and schools. An ethnographic portrait.* New York: Teachers College Press. [2]

Weiss, H.B., M. Caspe, & M.E. Lopez. 2006. *Family involvement in early childhood education.* Cambridge, MA: Harvard Family Research Project. [2]

Xu, Y., & J. Filler. 2008. Facilitating family involvement and support for inclusive education. *The School Community Journal* 18 (2): 53–71. [2]

Standard 3: Observing, Documenting, and Assessing to Support Young Children and Families

Cohen, D.H., V. Stern, N. Balaban, & N. Gropper. 2008. *Observing and recording the behavior of young children.* 5th ed. New York: Teachers College Press. [3]

DEC (Division for Early Childhood). 2007. Promoting positive outcomes for children with disabilities: Recommendations for curriculum, assessment, and program evaluation. Missoula, MT: Author. http://www.naeyc.org/files/naeyc/file/positions/PrmtgPositiveOutcomes.pdf [3]

Gonzales-Meña, J. 2005. *Resources for observation and reflection to accompany foundations of early childhood education.* New York: McGraw Hill [3]

Kagan, S.L., C. Scott-Little, & R.M. Clifford. 2003. Assessing young children: What policy makers need to know and do. In *Assessing the state of state assessments: Perspectives on assessing young children*, eds C. Scott-Little, S.L. Kagan, & R.M. Clifford, 25–35. Greensboro, NC: SERVE. [3]

Lynch, E., & M. Hanson. 2004. Family diversity assessment and cultural competence. In *Assessing infants and preschoolers with special needs*, 3rd ed., eds. M. McLean, D.B. Bailey, & M. Wolery, 71–99. Columbus, OH: Merrill/Pearson. [3]

Meisels, S.J., & S. Atkins-Burnett. 2000. The elements of early childhood assessment. In *Handbook of early childhood intervention*, 2nd ed., eds. J.P. Shonkoff & S.J. Meisels, 387–415. New York: Cambridge University Press. [3]

NAEYC. 2005. Screening and assessment of young English-language learners: Supplement to the NAEYC and NAECS/SDE [National Association of Early Childhood Specialists in State Departments of Education] joint position statement on early childhood curriculum, assessment, and program evaluation. http://www.naeyc.org/files/naeyc/file/positions/ELL_Supplement_Shorter_Version.pdf [3, 4]

NAEYC & NAECS/SDE. 2003. Early childhood curriculum, assessment, and program evaluation: Building an effective, accountable system in programs for children birth through age 8. Joint position statement. http://www.naeyc.org/files/naeyc/file/positions/CAPEexpand.pdf [3]

National Research Council. 2008. *Early childhood assessment: Why, what, and how.* Eds. C.E. Snow & S.B. Van Hemel, Committee on Developmental Outcomes and Assessments for Young Children; Board on Children, Youth, and Families & Board on Testing and Assessment, Division of Behavioral and Social Sciences and Education. Washington, DC: National Academies Press. [3]

Standard 4: Teaching Methods and Strategies

August, D., & T. Shanahan. 2006. *Developing literacy in second-language learners: Report of the National Literacy Panel on Language-Minority Children and Youth.* Mahwah, NJ: Erlbaum. [4, 5]

Burchinal, M., C. Howes, R. Pianta, D. Bryant, D. Early, R. Clifford, & O. Barbarin. 2008. Predicting child outcomes at the end of kindergarten from the quality of pre-kindergarten teacher-child interactions and instructions. *Applied Developmental Science* 12 (3): 140–53. [4]

Harowitz, F.D., F. Darling Hammond, J. Bransford, et al. 2005. Educating teachers for developmentally appropriate practice. In *Preparing teachers for a changing world: What teachers should learn and be able to do*, eds. L. Darling-Hammond & J. Bransford, 88–125. San Francisco: Jossey-Bass. [4]

Hemmeter, M.L., R.M. Santos, & M.M. Ostrosky. 2008. Preparing early childhood educators to address young children's social-emotional development and challenging behaviors. *Journal of Early Intervention* 30 (4): 321–40. [4]

Hirsh-Pasek, K., R.M. Golinkoff, L.E. Berk, & D.G. Singer. 2009. *A mandate for playful learning in preschool: Presenting the evidence.* New York: Oxford University Press. [4]

Howes, C., & S. Ritchie. 2002. *A matter of trust: Connecting teachers and learners in the early childhood classroom.* New York: Teachers College Press. [4]

Hyson, M. 2008. *Enthusiastic and engaged learners: Approaches to learning in the early childhood classroom.* New York: Teachers College. [4]

Mouza, C. 2005. Using technology to enhance early childhood learning: The 100 Days of School project. *Educational Research and Evaluation* 11 (6): 513–28. [4]

Pellegrini, A.D., L. Gada, M. Bartinin, & D. Charak. 1998. Oral language and literacy learning in context: The role of social relationships. *Merrill-Palmer Quarterly* 44 (1): 38–54. [4]

Saracho, O.N., & B. Spodek. 2008. *Contemporary perspectives on science and technology in early childhood education.* Charlotte, NC: Information Age Publishing. [4, 5]

Standard 5: Curriculum

Bae, J. 2004. Learning to teach visual arts in an early childhood classroom: The teacher's role as a guide. *Early Childhood Education Journal* 31 (4): 247–54. [5]

Bodrova, E., & D.L. Leong. 2005. Self-regulation: A foundation for early learning. *Principal* 85 (1): 30–35. [5]

Clements, D.H., J. Sarama, & A.M. DiBiase. 2004. *Engaging young children in mathematics: Standards for early childhood mathematics education.* Mahwah, NJ: Lawrence Erlbaum. [5]

Derman Sparks, L., & J. Olsen Edwards. 2009. *Anti-bias education for young children and ourselves.* Washington, DC: NAEYC. [5]

Dickinson, D.K., & P.O. Tabors. 2001. *Beginning literacy with language: Young children learning at home and school.* Baltimore, MD: Brookes. [4, 5]

Gelman, R., & K. Brenneman. 2004. Science learning pathways for young children. *Early Childhood Research Quarterly* 19 (2): 150–58. [5]

Ginsburg, H.P., J.S. Lee, & J.S. Boyd. 2008. Mathematics education for young children: What it is and how to promote it. *Social Policy Report* 22 (1): 3–11, 14–22. [5]

Hyson, M. 2004. *The emotional development of young children: Building an emotion-centered curriculum.* 2nd ed. New York: Teachers College Press. [5]

Mindes, G. 2005. Social studies in today's early childhood curricula. *Young Children* 60 (5): 12–18. [5]

National Early Literacy Panel. 2008. *Developing early literacy: Report of the National Early Literacy Panel—A scientific synthesis of early literacy development and implications for intervention.* Washington, DC: National Institute for Literacy. [5]

National Mathematics Advisory Panel. 2008. *Foundations for success: The Final Report of the National Mathematics Advisory Panel.* Washington, DC: U.S. Department of Education [5]

Sanders, S.W. 2006. Physical education in kindergarten. In *K today: Teaching and learning in the kindergarten year,* ed. D.F. Gullow, 127–37. Washington, DC: NAEYC. [5]

Singer, M.J. 2008. Accessing the musical intelligence in early childhood education. *Australian Journal of Early Childhood* 33 (2): 49–56. [5]

Standard 6: Becoming a Professional

Baptiste, N.E., & L.C. Reyes. 2008. *What every teacher should know about understanding ethics in early care and education.* 3rd ed. Upper Saddle River, NJ: Prentice Hall. [6]

Division for Early Childhood (DEC). 2009. *Code of ethics.* Retrieved August 27, 2009, at www.dec-sped.org/uploads/docs/about_dec/position_concept_papers/Code%20of%20Ethics_updated_Aug2009.pdf [6]

Freeman, N.K., & K.J. Swick. 2007. The ethical dimension of working with parents: Using the code of ethics when faced with a difficult decision. *Childhood Education* 83 (3): 163–69. [6]

Hurst, B., & G. Reding. 2009. *Professionalism in teaching. What every teacher should know about.* 2nd ed. Columbus, OH: Merrill/Pearson. [6]

Kagan, S.L., K. Kauerz, & K. Tarrant. 2007. *The early care and education teaching workforce at the fulcrum: An agenda for reform.* New York: Teachers College Press. [6]

NAEYC. 2004. *Code of ethical conduct: Supplement for early childhood adult educators. A joint position statement of NAEYC, NAECTE (National Association of Early Childhood Teacher Educators), & ACCESS (American Associate Degree Early Childhood Teacher Educators).* http://www.naeyc.org/files/nacyc/file/positions/ethics04.pdf [6]

NAEYC. 2005. *Code of ethical conduct and statement of commitment. A position statement of the National Association for the Education of Young Children.* Brochure. Washington, DC: Author. [6]

NAEYC. 2006. Code of ethical conduct: Supplement for early childhood program administrators. A position statement. http://www.naeyc.org/files/naeyc/file/positions/Supplement%20PS2011.pdf [6]

Paige-Smith, A., & A. Craft. 2008. *Developing reflective practice in the early years.* England: Open University Press. [6]

Rust, F., & E. Meyers. 2006. The bright side: Teacher research in the context of educational reform and policy making. *Teachers & Teaching* 12 (1): 69–86. [6]

Wesley, P.W., & V. Buysee. 2006. Ethics and evidence in consultation. *Topics in Early Childhood Special Education* 26 (3): 131–41. [6]

Winton, P.J., J.A. McCollum, & C. Catlett, eds. 2007. *Practical approaches to early childhood professional development: Evidence, strategies, and resources.* Washington, DC: Zero to Three.

Zaslow, M., & I. Martinez-Beck, eds. 2005. *Critical issues in early childhood professional development.* Baltimore, MD: Brookes.

The 2008–2009 Standards Work Group

Becky Brinks
Child Development Program Director, Grand Rapids Community College, Michigan
Chair, Commission on NAEYC Early Childhood Associate Degree Accreditation

Julie Bullard
Director, Early Childhood Education, University of Montana–Western, Dillon, Montana
NAEYC Reviewer and Audit Team member, NCATE

Josué Cruz Jr.
President and CEO, Council for Professional Recognition, Washington, D.C.

Sharon Fredericks
Education Division Director/Instructor, College of Menominee Nation, Green Bay, Wisconsin
Community College faculty in ECADA Self Study, Head Start Higher Education Grantee

John Johnston
Professor and Director of Assessment, College of Education, University of Memphis, Tennessee
NAEYC Reviewer, Audit Team, and Specialty Areas Standards Board member, NCATE

Frances O'Connell Rust
Senior Vice President for Academic Affairs, Dean of Faculty, Erikson Institute, Chicago, Illinois

Ursula Thomas-Fair
Assistant Professor, University of West Georgia, Carrollton, Georgia

Contents

Code of Ethical Conduct
and Statement of Commitment

Revised April 2005,
Reaffirmed and Updated May 2011
Endorsed by the Association for Childhood Education International
Adopted by the National Association for Family Child Care

Preamble

NAEYC recognizes that those who work with young children face many daily decisions that have moral and ethical implications. The **NAEYC Code of Ethical Conduct** offers guidelines for responsible behavior and sets forth a common basis for resolving the principal ethical dilemmas encountered in early childhood care and education. The **Statement of Commitment** is not part of the Code but is a personal acknowledgement of an individual's willingness to embrace the distinctive values and moral obligations of the field of early childhood care and education.

The primary focus of the Code is on daily practice with children and their families in programs for children from birth through 8 years of age, such as infant/toddler programs, preschool and prekindergarten programs, child care centers, hospital and child life settings, family child care homes, kindergartens, and primary classrooms. When the issues involve young children, then these provisions also apply to specialists who do not work directly with children, including program administrators, parent educators, early childhood adult educators, and officials with responsibility for program monitoring and licensing. (Note: See also the "Code of Ethical Conduct: Supplement for Early Childhood Adult Educators," online at http://www.naeyc.org/files/naeyc/file/positions/ethics04.pdf and the "Code of Ethical Conduct: Supplement for Early Childhood Program Administrators," online at http://www.naeyc.org/files/naeyc/file/positions/Supplement%20PS2011.pdf.)

Core values

Standards of ethical behavior in early childhood care and education are based on commitment to the following core values that are deeply rooted in the history of the field of early childhood care and education. We have made a commitment to

• Appreciate childhood as a unique and valuable stage of the human life cycle

• Base our work on knowledge of how children develop and learn

• Appreciate and support the bond between the child and family

* The term *culture* includes ethnicity, racial identity, economic level, family structure, language, and religious and political beliefs, which profoundly influence each child's development and relationship to the world.

- Recognize that children are best understood and supported in the context of family, culture,* community, and society
- Respect the dignity, worth, and uniqueness of each individual (child, family member, and colleague)
- Respect diversity in children, families, and colleagues
- Recognize that children and adults achieve their full potential in the context of relationships that are based on trust and respect

Conceptual framework

The Code sets forth a framework of professional responsibilities in four sections. Each section addresses an area of professional relationships: (1) with children, (2) with families, (3) among colleagues, and (4) with the community and society. Each section includes an introduction to the primary responsibilities of the early childhood practitioner in that context. The introduction is followed by a set of ideals (I) that reflect exemplary professional practice and by a set of principles (P) describing practices that are required, prohibited, or permitted.

The **ideals** reflect the aspirations of practitioners. The **principles** guide conduct and assist practitioners in resolving ethical dilemmas.* Both ideals and principles are intended to direct practitioners to those questions which, when responsibly answered, can provide the basis for conscientious decision making. While the Code provides specific direction for addressing some ethical dilemmas, many others will require the practitioner to combine the guidance of the Code with professional judgment.

The ideals and principles in this Code present a shared framework of professional responsibility that affirms our commitment to the core values of our field. The Code publicly acknowledges the responsibilities that we in the field have assumed, and in so doing supports ethical behavior in our work. Practitioners who face situations with ethical dimensions are urged to seek guidance in the applicable parts of this Code and in the spirit that informs the whole.

Often "the right answer"—the best ethical course of action to take—is not obvious. There may be no readily apparent, positive way to handle

* There is not necessarily a corresponding principle for each ideal.

a situation. When one important value contradicts another, we face an ethical dilemma. When we face a dilemma, it is our professional responsibility to consult the Code and all relevant parties to find the most ethical resolution.

Section I
Ethical responsibilities to children

Childhood is a unique and valuable stage in the human life cycle. Our paramount responsibility is to provide care and education in settings that are safe, healthy, nurturing, and responsive for each child. We are committed to supporting children's development and learning; respecting individual differences; and helping children learn to live, play, and work cooperatively. We are also committed to promoting children's self-awareness, competence, self-worth, resiliency, and physical well-being.

Ideals

I-1.1—To be familiar with the knowledge base of early childhood care and education and to stay informed through continuing education and training.

I-1.2—To base program practices upon current knowledge and research in the field of early childhood education, child development, and related disciplines, as well as on particular knowledge of each child.

I-1.3—To recognize and respect the unique qualities, abilities, and potential of each child.

I-1.4—To appreciate the vulnerability of children and their dependence on adults.

I-1.5—To create and maintain safe and healthy settings that foster children's social, emotional, cognitive, and physical development and that respect their dignity and their contributions.

I-1.6—To use assessment instruments and strategies that are appropriate for the children to be assessed, that are used only for the purposes for which they were designed, and that have the potential to benefit children.

I-1.7—To use assessment information to understand and support children's development and learning, to support instruction, and to identify children who may need additional services.

I-1.8—To support the right of each child to play and learn in an inclusive environment that meets the needs of children with and without disabilities.

I-1.9—To advocate for and ensure that all children, including those with special needs, have access to the support services needed to be successful.

I-1.10—To ensure that each child's culture, language, ethnicity, and family structure are recognized and valued in the program.

I-1.11—To provide all children with experiences in a language that they know, as well as support children in maintaining the use of their home language and in learning English.

I-1.12—To work with families to provide a safe and smooth transition as children and families move from one program to the next.

Principles

P-1.1—Above all, we shall not harm children. We shall not participate in practices that are emotionally damaging, physically harmful, disrespectful, degrading, dangerous, exploitative, or intimidating to children. *This principle has precedence over all others in this Code.*

P-1.2—We shall care for and educate children in positive emotional and social environments that are cognitively stimulating and that support each child's culture, language, ethnicity, and family structure.

P-1.3—We shall not participate in practices that discriminate against children by denying benefits, giving special advantages, or excluding them from programs or activities on the basis of their sex, race, national origin, immigration status, preferred home language, religious beliefs, medical condition, disability, or the marital status/family structure, sexual orientation, or religious beliefs or other affiliations of their families. (Aspects of this principle do not apply in programs that have a lawful mandate to provide services to a particular population of children.)

P-1.4—We shall use two-way communications to involve all those with relevant knowledge (including families and staff) in decisions concerning a child, as appropriate, ensuring confidentiality of sensitive information. (See also P-2.4.)

P-1.5—We shall use appropriate assessment systems, which include multiple sources of information, to provide information on children's learning and development.

P-1.6—We shall strive to ensure that decisions such as those related to enrollment, retention, or assignment to special education services, will be based on multiple sources of information

and will never be based on a single assessment, such as a test score or a single observation.

P-1.7—We shall strive to build individual relationships with each child; make individualized adaptations in teaching strategies, learning environments, and curricula; and consult with the family so that each child benefits from the program. If after such efforts have been exhausted, the current placement does not meet a child's needs, or the child is seriously jeopardizing the ability of other children to benefit from the program, we shall collaborate with the child's family and appropriate specialists to determine the additional services needed and/or the placement option(s) most likely to ensure the child's success. (Aspects of this principle may not apply in programs that have a lawful mandate to provide services to a particular population of children.)

P-1.8—We shall be familiar with the risk factors for and symptoms of child abuse and neglect, including physical, sexual, verbal, and emotional abuse and physical, emotional, educational, and medical neglect. We shall know and follow state laws and community procedures that protect children against abuse and neglect.

P-1.9—When we have reasonable cause to suspect child abuse or neglect, we shall report it to the appropriate community agency and follow up to ensure that appropriate action has been taken. When appropriate, parents or guardians will be informed that the referral will be or has been made.

P-1.10—When another person tells us of his or her suspicion that a child is being abused or neglected, we shall assist that person in taking appropriate action in order to protect the child.

P-1.11—When we become aware of a practice or situation that endangers the health, safety, or well-being of children, we have an ethical responsibility to protect children or inform parents and/or others who can.

Section II

Ethical responsibilities to families

Families* are of primary importance in children's development. Because the family and the early childhood practitioner have a common interest in the child's well-being, we acknowledge a primary responsibility to bring about communication, cooperation, and collaboration between the home and early childhood program in ways that enhance the child's development.

Ideals

I-2.1—To be familiar with the knowledge base related to working effectively with families and to stay informed through continuing education and training.

I-2.2—To develop relationships of mutual trust and create partnerships with the families we serve.

I-2.3—To welcome all family members and encourage them to participate in the program, including involvement in shared decision making.

I-2.4—To listen to families, acknowledge and build upon their strengths and competencies, and learn from families as we support them in their task of nurturing children.

I-2.5—To respect the dignity and preferences of each family and to make an effort to learn about its structure, culture, language, customs, and beliefs to ensure a culturally consistent environment for all children and families.

I-2.6—To acknowledge families' childrearing values and their right to make decisions for their children.

I-2.7—To share information about each child's education and development with families and to help them understand and appreciate the current knowledge base of the early childhood profession.

I-2.8—To help family members enhance their understanding of their children, as staff are enhancing their understanding of each child through communications with families, and support family members in the continuing development of their skills as parents.

I-2.9—To foster families' efforts to build support networks and, when needed, participate in building networks for families by providing them with opportunities to interact with program staff, other families, community resources, and professional services.

Principles

P-2.1—We shall not deny family members access to their child's classroom or program setting unless access is denied by court order or other legal restriction.

P-2.2—We shall inform families of program philosophy, policies, curriculum, assessment system, cultural practices, and personnel qualifications, and explain why we teach as we do—which should be in accordance with our ethical responsibilities to children (see Section I).

P-2.3—We shall inform families of and, when appropriate, involve them in policy decisions. (See also I-2.3.)

P-2.4—We shall ensure that the family is involved in significant decisions affecting their child. (See also P-1.4.)

P-2.5—We shall make every effort to communicate effectively with all families in a language that they understand. We shall use community resources for translation and interpretation when we do not have sufficient resources in our own programs.

P-2.6—As families share information with us about their children and families, we shall ensure that families' input is an important contribution to the planning and implementation of the program.

P-2.7—We shall inform families about the nature and purpose of the program's child assessments and how data about their child will be used.

P-2.8—We shall treat child assessment information confidentially and share this information only when there is a legitimate need for it.

P-2.9—We shall inform the family of injuries and incidents involving their child, of risks such as exposures to communicable diseases that might result in infection, and of occurrences that might result in emotional stress.

P-2.10—Families shall be fully informed of any proposed research projects involving their children and shall have the opportunity to give or withhold consent without penalty. We shall not permit or participate in research that could in any way hinder the education, development, or well-being of children.

P-2.11—We shall not engage in or support exploitation of families. We shall not use our relationship with a family for private advantage or personal gain, or enter into relationships with family members that might impair our effectiveness working with their children.

P-2.12—We shall develop written policies for the protection of confidentiality and the disclosure of children's records. These policy documents shall be made available to all program personnel and families. Disclosure of children's

---

* The term *family* may include those adults, besides parents, with the responsibility of being involved in educating, nurturing, and advocating for the child.

records beyond family members, program personnel, and consultants having an obligation of confidentiality shall require familial consent (except in cases of abuse or neglect).

P-2.13—We shall maintain confidentiality and shall respect the family's right to privacy, refraining from disclosure of confidential information and intrusion into family life. However, when we have reason to believe that a child's welfare is at risk, it is permissible to share confidential information with agencies, as well as with individuals who have legal responsibility for intervening in the child's interest.

P-2.14—In cases where family members are in conflict with one another, we shall work openly, sharing our observations of the child, to help all parties involved make informed decisions. We shall refrain from becoming an advocate for one party.

P-2.15—We shall be familiar with and appropriately refer families to community resources and professional support services. After a referral has been made, we shall follow up to ensure that services have been appropriately provided.

Section III

Ethical responsibilities to colleagues

In a caring, cooperative workplace, human dignity is respected, professional satisfaction is promoted, and positive relationships are developed and sustained. Based upon our core values, our primary responsibility to colleagues is to establish and maintain settings and relationships that support productive work and meet professional needs. The same ideals that apply to children also apply as we interact with adults in the workplace. (Note: Section III includes responsibilities to co-workers and to employers. See the "Code of Ethical Conduct: Supplement for Early Childhood Program Administrators" for responsibilities to personnel (*employees* in the original 2005 Code revision), online at http://www.naeyc.org/files/naeyc/file/positions/Supplement%20PS2011.pdf.)

A—Responsibilities to co-workers

Ideals

I-3A.1—To establish and maintain relationships of respect, trust, confidentiality, collaboration, and cooperation with co-workers.

I-3A.2—To share resources with co-workers, collaborating to ensure that the best possible early childhood care and education program is provided.

I-3A.3—To support co-workers in meeting their professional needs and in their professional development.

I-3A.4—To accord co-workers due recognition of professional achievement.

Principles

P-3A.1—We shall recognize the contributions of colleagues to our program and not participate in practices that diminish their reputations or impair their effectiveness in working with children and families.

P-3A.2—When we have concerns about the professional behavior of a co-worker, we shall first let that person know of our concern in a way that shows respect for personal dignity and for the diversity to be found among staff members, and then attempt to resolve the matter collegially and in a confidential manner.

P-3A.3—We shall exercise care in expressing views regarding the personal attributes or professional conduct of co-workers. Statements should be based on firsthand knowledge, not hearsay, and relevant to the interests of children and programs.

P-3A.4—We shall not participate in practices that discriminate against a co-worker because of sex, race, national origin, religious beliefs or other affiliations, age, marital status/family structure, disability, or sexual orientation.

B—Responsibilities to employers

Ideals

I-3B.1—To assist the program in providing the highest quality of service.

I-3B.2—To do nothing that diminishes the reputation of the program in which we work unless it is violating laws and regulations designed to protect children or is violating the provisions of this Code.

Principles

P-3B.1—We shall follow all program policies. When we do not agree with program policies, we shall attempt to effect change through constructive action within the organization.

P-3B.2—We shall speak or act on behalf of an organization only when authorized. We shall take care to acknowledge when we are speaking for the organization and when we are expressing a personal judgment.

P-3B.3—We shall not violate laws or regulations designed to protect children and shall take appropriate action consistent with this Code when aware of such violations.

P-3B.4—If we have concerns about a colleague's behavior, and children's well-being is not at risk, we may address the concern with that individual. If children are at risk or the situation does not improve after it has been brought to the colleague's attention, we shall report the colleague's unethical or incompetent behavior to an appropriate authority.

P-3B.5—When we have a concern about circumstances or conditions that impact the quality of care and education within the program, we shall inform the program's administration or, when necessary, other appropriate authorities.

Section IV

Ethical responsibilities to community and society

Early childhood programs operate within the context of their immediate community made up of families and other institutions concerned with children's welfare. Our responsibilities to the community are to provide programs that meet the diverse needs of families, to cooperate with agencies and professions that share the responsibility for children, to assist families in gaining access to those agencies and allied professionals, and to assist in the development of community programs that are needed but not currently available.

As individuals, we acknowledge our responsibility to provide the best possible programs of care and education for children and to conduct ourselves with honesty and integrity. Because of our specialized expertise in early childhood development and education and because the larger society shares responsibility for the welfare and protection of young children, we acknowledge a collective obligation to advocate for the best interests of children within early childhood programs and in the larger community and to serve as a voice for young children everywhere.

The ideals and principles in this section are presented to distinguish between those that pertain to the work of the individual early childhood educator and those that more typically are engaged in collectively on behalf of the best interests of children—with the understanding that individual early childhood educators have a shared responsibility for addressing the ideals and principles that are identified as "collective."

Ideal (Individual)

I-4.1—To provide the community with high-quality early childhood care and education programs and services.

Ideals (Collective)

I-4.2—To promote cooperation among professionals and agencies and interdisciplinary collaboration among professions concerned with addressing issues in the health, education, and well-being of young children, their families, and their early childhood educators.

I-4.3—To work through education, research, and advocacy toward an environmentally safe world in which all children receive health care, food, and shelter; are nurtured; and live free from violence in their home and their communities.

I-4.4—To work through education, research, and advocacy toward a society in which all young children have access to high-quality early care and education programs.

I-4.5—To work to ensure that appropriate assessment systems, which include multiple sources of information, are used for purposes that benefit children.

I-4.6—To promote knowledge and understanding of young children and their needs. To work toward greater societal acknowledgment of children's rights and greater social acceptance of responsibility for the well-being of all children.

I-4.7—To support policies and laws that promote the well-being of children and families, and to work to change those that impair their well-being. To participate in developing policies and laws that are needed, and to cooperate with families and other individuals and groups in these efforts.

I-4.8—To further the professional development of the field of early childhood care and education and to strengthen its commitment to realizing its core values as reflected in this Code.

Principles (Individual)

P-4.1—We shall communicate openly and truthfully about the nature and extent of services that we provide.

P-4.2—We shall apply for, accept, and work in positions for which we are personally well-suited and professionally qualified. We shall not offer services that we do not have the competence, qualifications, or resources to provide.

P-4.3—We shall carefully check references and shall not hire or recommend for employment any person whose competence, qualifications, or character makes him or her unsuited for the position.

P-4.4—We shall be objective and accurate in reporting the knowledge upon which we base our program practices.

P-4.5—We shall be knowledgeable about the appropriate use of assessment strategies and instruments and interpret results accurately to families.

P-4.6—We shall be familiar with laws and regulations that serve to protect the children in our programs and be vigilant in ensuring that these laws and regulations are followed.

P-4.7—When we become aware of a practice or situation that endangers the health, safety, or well-being of children, we have an ethical responsibility to protect children or inform parents and/or others who can.

P-4.8—We shall not participate in practices that are in violation of laws and regulations that protect the children in our programs.

P-4.9—When we have evidence that an early childhood program is violating laws or regulations protecting children, we shall report the violation to appropriate authorities who can be expected to remedy the situation.

P-4.10—When a program violates or requires its employees to violate this Code, it is permissible, after fair assessment of the evidence, to disclose the identity of that program.

Principles (Collective)

P-4.11—When policies are enacted for purposes that do not benefit children, we have a collective responsibility to work to change these policies.

P-4.12—When we have evidence that an agency that provides services intended to ensure children's well-being is failing to meet its obligations, we acknowledge a collective ethical responsibility to report the problem to appropriate authorities or to the public. We shall be vigilant in our follow-up until the situation is resolved.

P-4.13—When a child protection agency fails to provide adequate protection for abused or neglected children, we acknowledge a collective ethical responsibility to work toward the improvement of these services.

NAEYC Code of Ethical Conduct 2005 Revisions Workgroup

Mary Ambery, Ruth Ann Ball, James Clay, Julie Olsen Edwards, Harriet Egertson, Anthony Fair, Stephanie Feeney, Jana Fleming, Nancy Freeman, Marla Israel, Allison McKinnon, Evelyn Wright Moore, Eva Moravcik, Christina Lopez Morgan, Sarah Mulligan, Nila Rinehart, Betty Holston Smith, and Peter Pizzolongo, NAEYC Staff

Glossary of Terms Related to Ethics

Code of Ethics. Defines the core values of the field and provides guidance for what professionals should do when they encounter conflicting obligations or responsibilities in their work.

Values. Qualities or principles that individuals believe to be desirable or worthwhile and that they prize for themselves, for others, and for the world in which they live.

Core Values. Commitments held by a profession that are consciously and knowingly embraced by its practitioners because they make a contribution to society. There is a difference between personal values and the core values of a profession.

Morality. Peoples' views of what is good, right, and proper; their beliefs about their obligations; and their ideas about how they should behave.

Ethics. The study of right and wrong, or duty and obligation, that involves critical reflection on morality and the ability to make choices between values and the examination of the moral dimensions of relationships.

Professional Ethics. The moral commitments of a profession that involve moral reflection that extends and enhances the personal morality practitioners bring to their work, that concern actions of right and wrong in the workplace, and that help individuals resolve moral dilemmas they encounter in their work.

Ethical Responsibilities. Behaviors that one must or must not engage in. Ethical responsibilities are clear-cut and are spelled out in the Code of Ethical Conduct (for example, early childhood educators should never share confidential information about a child or family with a person who has no legitimate need for knowing).

Ethical Dilemma. A moral conflict that involves determining appropriate conduct when an individual faces conflicting professional values and responsibilities.

Sources for glossary terms and definitions

Feeney, S., & N. Freeman. 2005. *Ethics and the early childhood educator: Using the NAEYC code.* Washington, DC: NAEYC.

Kidder, R.M. 1995. *How good people make tough choices: Resolving the dilemmas of ethical living.* New York: Fireside.

Kipnis, K. 1987. How to discuss professional ethics. *Young Children* 42 (4): 26–30.

Statement of Commitment*

As an individual who works with young children, I commit myself to furthering the values of early childhood education as they are reflected in the ideals and principles of the NAEYC Code of Ethical Conduct. To the best of my ability I will

• Never harm children.

• Ensure that programs for young children are based on current knowledge and research of child development and early childhood education.

• Respect and support families in their task of nurturing children.

• Respect colleagues in early childhood care and education and support them in maintaining the NAEYC Code of Ethical Conduct.

• Serve as an advocate for children, their families, and their teachers in community and society.

• Stay informed of and maintain high standards of professional conduct.

• Engage in an ongoing process of self-reflection, realizing that personal characteristics, biases, and beliefs have an impact on children and families.

• Be open to new ideas and be willing to learn from the suggestions of others.

• Continue to learn, grow, and contribute as a professional.

• Honor the ideals and principles of the NAEYC Code of Ethical Conduct.

* This Statement of Commitment is not part of the Code but is a personal acknowledgment of the individual's willingness to embrace the distinctive values and moral obligations of the field of early childhood care and education. It is recognition of the moral obligations that lead to an individual becoming part of the profession.

Contents

Code of Ethical Conduct
Supplement for Early Childhood Adult Educators

Adopted Spring 2004.

A Joint Position Statement of
the National Association for the Education of Young Children (NAEYC),
the National Association of Early Childhood Teacher Educators (NAECTE), and
American Associate Degree Early Childhood Teacher Educators (ACCESS)

Adopted by the National Association for Family Child Care

Early childhood educators who teach adults to work in early childhood settings are called upon to sustain different relationships and to balance the needs of a wider variety of clients than those who work directly with young children and their families. And as teacher educators fulfill their responsibilities to adult learners, they encounter some unique ethical challenges in the context of a complex network of relationships. The primary challenge is to find a balance between an obligation to support and nurture adult learners and the obligation to provide caring and competent professionals to work with young children and their families. While the existing NAEYC Code of Ethical Conduct is a valuable resource that addresses many of the ethical issues encountered by early childhood adult educators, it does not provide all of the guidance they need to address the ethical issues that arise in their work.

Through this Supplement to the Code of Ethical Conduct, NAEYC, NAECTE, and ACCESS hope to identify and explore the recurring ethical dilemmas faced by early childhood adult educa-

tors, and to reach some consensus about how they might best be addressed. This Supplement places primary emphasis on the ethical responsibilities and recurring ethical dilemmas that face early childhood teacher educators in two- and four-year degree-granting institutions. However, many of its provisions are also applicable to early childhood educators who provide nondegree training and mentoring to adults in early childhood care and education settings.

Purpose of the supplement

Like those who work with young children, early childhood adult educators are regularly called upon to make decisions of a moral and ethical nature. The NAEYC Code of Ethical Conduct is a foundational document that maps the ethical dimensions of early childhood educators' work in early care and education programs. Adult educators share the ethical obligations assumed by all early childhood educators, reflected in the core values, ideals, and principles set forth in the

NAEYC Code. **We embrace the central commitment of the field of early care and education to the healthy development and welfare of young children. Everything we do in our role as educators of adults is intended to further this ultimate commitment.**

Early childhood adult educators have ethical responsibilities beyond those spelled out in the NAEYC Code. They have responsibilities to adult students; institutions of higher learning and agencies that conduct training; the programs in which they place adult students and staff and clientele; professional colleagues; children and their families and community; and society and the field of early childhood care and education at large.

Core values

In addition to adhering to the core values spelled out in the NAEYC Code of Ethical Conduct, early childhood adult educators commit themselves to the following two core values:

• To respect the critical role of a knowledgeable, competent, and diverse early childhood care and education workforce in supporting the development and learning of young children.

• To base practice on current and accurate knowledge of the fields of early childhood education, child development, adult development and learning, as well as other relevant disciplines.

Conceptual framework

This document sets forth a conception of early childhood teacher educators' professional responsibilities in six sections that address arenas of professional relationships. The sections are (1) adult learners, (2) sites providing practicum experiences, (3) employing institutions of higher learning and agencies that provide training, (4) professional colleagues, (5) children and families, and (6) community, society, and the field of early care and education. The first three sections address those areas of responsibility unique to educators who work primarily with adults. Sections 4-6 spell out additional responsibilities of early childhood adult educators in areas addressed in the NAEYC Code. When there is a direct parallel in the NAEYC Code or a related principle or ideal, the Code is referenced after the Supplement item.

Definitions

Early Childhood Adult Educator. A professional who teaches early childhood educators in an institution of higher education (includes adjunct faculty) and those who conduct not-for-credit training for the early care and education workforce.

Adult Learners. Adult learners, both pre-service and inservice, who work in or are preparing to work in settings that provide care and education for young children from birth through 8 years of age.

Student. An adult learner who is gaining pre-service or advanced education in the field of early childhood education and care through an educational institution.

Colleague. A fellow early childhood educator who teaches, trains, or mentors adult students in an institution of higher learning or who conducts not-for-credit training for the early education workforce. (*Note:* There are specific responsibilities to colleagues employed by one's own institution.)

Mentor. An experienced early childhood professional who works directly with both young children and practicum students in an early childhood program and who, in collaboration with an early childhood teacher educator, guides and counsels the students.

Ethics Supplement. Material that has been added to NAEYC Code of Ethical Conduct to provide further information and guidance about the ethical responsibilities of early childhood adult educators.

Ideals and principles

This Supplement to the NAEYC Code identifies additional ideals (aspirations) and principles (guides for conduct: definitions of practices that are required, prohibited, and permitted) that address the unique ethical responsibilities of early childhood adult educators. These ideals and principles were developed by analyzing adult educators' descriptions of recurring ethical dilemmas in their work. The goals and principles included in this Supplement are designed to inspire and guide early childhood adult educators toward actions that reflect the field's current understandings of their ethical responsibilities.

(*Note*: There is **not** a one-to-one correspondence between ideals and principles.)

1. Ethical responsibilities to adult learners

Our work is always guided by the core values of the field of early care and education, including our commitment to ensuring the welfare of children. From that perspective we prioritize the unique commitments of early childhood adult educators and acknowledge that our day-to-day responsibilities focus primarily on the professional development of adult learners.

Ideals

I–1.1—To continually update our own knowledge of the field of early care and education so that we are able to present current, well-grounded information to those we teach.

I–1.2—To provide college students with a foundation in core content areas of early childhood education, including child development and its social contexts; child guidance; the design of safe, healthy learning environments; curriculum and assessment; work with families; work with children and families from diverse cultures; advocacy skills; and professionalism, including ethics.

I–1.3—To provide adult learners with learning experiences based on principles of adult learning and consistent with the core values of early care and education, current knowledge, and best practices in the field.

I–1.4—To present controversial material fairly, acknowledging the validity of contrasting perspectives and, when appropriate, identifying our own biases.

I–1.5—To have high and reasonable expectations of learners.

I–1.6—To fairly and equitably assess what adult students know and are able to do.

I–1.7—To ensure that our programs serve diverse adult learners (including diversity in language, culture, race/ethnicity, and social class).

I–1.8—To ensure that our programs are accessible to those with diverse needs (as to the times, location, format, and language of training).

Principles

P–1.1—We shall provide learning experiences that are consistent with the best practices for adult learners and that match the needs, learning styles, cultures, and stages of development of adult learners.

P–1.2—We shall inform learners of conduct and work expectations, including institutional standards for writing, performance, and intellectual honesty.

P–1.3—We shall give learners a fair chance to succeed and diverse ways to demonstrate their competence.

P–1.4—We shall provide additional support for adult learners who have the potential to work effectively with young children but have difficulty meeting academic standards.

P–1.5—We shall provide additional support and counsel to those who demonstrate academic excellence while having difficulty in meeting standards for classroom practice.

P–1.6—We shall inform those seeking training in early childhood education of current economic and social conditions affecting the field so that they may make an educated decision about career choices.

P–1.7—We shall provide information about disparities between best practice and commonly accepted practice to better prepare students to face ongoing challenges related to their work with children.

P–1.8—We shall not place students or allow students to continue in placements that, in our best professional judgment, are not beneficial to children.

P–1.9—When it becomes apparent that a practicum placement is not supporting a student's professional development or is not beneficial to the student or children, every effort shall be made to move the student to a more appropriate placement.

P–1.10—When it becomes apparent that an adult learner is not able to benefit from our training, class, or program, we shall help her/him identify an alternative educational path or goal.

P–1.11—We shall honor confidentiality, sharing only necessary information about an adult learner, only to those who need to know, and only through appropriate professional channels.

P–1.12—We shall make it clear at the outset if training involves the sale of products or services from which we stand to gain financially and will do this only if the products or services are relevant and serve educational goals.

2. Ethical responsibilities to practicum sites

Some knowledge and skills needed by early childhood educators can only be acquired through direct experience in early childhood settings. Therefore, early childhood adult educators rely heavily on placements in programs (practicum sites) in which students can apply what they have learned, get feedback from children and adults, and reflect on what they have learned from their experience.

Ideals

I–2.1—To provide practicum experiences that will positively support the professional development of adult students.

I–2.2—To foster collegial and collaborative working relationships with educators who work in practicum settings.

I–2.3—To be respectful of the responsibilities, expertise, and perspective of practitioners who work with students in practicum settings.

I–2.4—To recognize the importance and contributions of practicum staff members in the professional development of our students.

Principles

P–2.1—We shall place students in settings where staff are qualified to work with young children, where mentors have experience and training in supporting adult learners, and which to the greatest extent possible reflect the diverse communities in which our students will be working.

P–2.2—We shall clearly state all parties' roles and responsibilities and prepare students, mentors, and administrators for practicum experiences. We shall provide appropriate support for all parties' efforts to fulfill their roles and meet program expectations.

P–2.3—When we have a concern about a program in which we place students, we shall address that concern with the classroom teacher or program administrator. (If the concerns relate to the health or safety of children, see the applicable sections of the NAEYC Code: P-1.11 and P-4.9-12.)

P–2.4—We shall ensure that qualified personnel conduct regular supervision of practicum experiences in order to support professional development of adult students and monitor the welfare of children.

P–2.5—We shall honor confidentiality and guard the privacy of the programs (teachers and clientele) in which we place students.

P–2.6—We shall teach adult students that they have a professional obligation to honor confidentiality and shall make every effort to ensure that they guard the privacy of the program, its teachers, and clientele.

3. Ethical obligations to institutions of higher learning and agencies providing training

Our primary responsibility to our employers is the development of knowledge and skill in adult learners. This work is intended to further our ultimate commitment to the welfare and development of young children. (Section III-B of the NAEYC Code provides the foundation for the additional commitments for adult educators listed below.)

Ideals

I–3.1—To assist the institutions and agencies for whom we work in providing the highest quality of educational programs for adult learners. (NAEYC Code I-3B.1)

Principles

P–3.1—We shall respect the integrity of courses by following approved course descriptions.

P–3.2—We shall evaluate our adult learners fairly, using those standards that are congruent with the mission of our institution and regarded as accepted practice in the field.

P–3.3—We shall offer training and instruction only in areas in which we have or can obtain appropriate experience and expertise. (NAEYC Code P-4.2)

P–3.4—We shall, when our involvement with a student involves more than one role (e.g., instructor, employer, supervisor), keep these roles separate. We shall make decisions, recommendations, and give feedback appropriate to the different contexts.

4. Ethical responsibilities regarding colleagues

The work of the early childhood adult educator involves interaction and collaboration with colleagues. Our professional responsibility to colleagues is to maintain positive and productive working relationships. (Section III-A of the NAEYC Code provides the foundation for the additional commitments for adult educators listed below.)

Ideals

I–4.1—To be collegial to and supportive of early childhood coworkers in our own and other institutions. (NAEYC Code I-3A.1-4)

I–4.2—To serve as mentors to junior faculty and novice adult educators.

Principles

P–4.1—When an adult learner comes to us with concerns about a colleague's competence, fairness, ethics, or accuracy, we will give the learner support in clarifying his or her concerns and in deciding and following through on a course of action to address the problem.

P–4.2—When we have concerns regarding a colleague's competence, fairness, ethics, or accuracy, we will *first* express our concerns to that colleague. (NAEYC Code P-3A.2)

P–4.3—When a colleague appears unwilling or unable to address problems, we will express our opinions about his or her competence through official channels such as performance evaluation.

P–4.4—We shall honor confidentiality and share information about colleagues in appropriate institutional settings. We shall not share information about colleagues in the community or with students.

5. Ethical responsibilities to children and families

Because those we train have a direct impact on children's lives, early childhood adult educators have some additional responsibilities to children and families above and beyond what is set forth in the NAEYC Code of Ethical Conduct.

Ideals

I–5.1—To support the development of competent and caring professionals to work with young children and their families.

I–5.2—To provide a diverse workforce that reflects the linguistic, racial/ethnic, cultural, and socioeconomic backgrounds of the children served in early childhood programs and their communities.

I–5.3—To speak out against practices that are unjust or harmful to young children and their families.

Principles

P–5.1—We shall make the welfare of children the deciding factor in our decisions regarding our work with adult learners. We shall not participate in or overlook practices (in our students, colleagues, institutions, agencies, or practicum settings) that are harmful to children. **This principle has precedence over all others in this Supplement.** (NAEYC Code P-1.1)

P–5.2—We shall provide sound educational experiences for those we teach that enable them to understand and provide for the optimal development of children and support for their families.

P–5.3—We shall not allow a student to complete a program if we have direct evidence that he/she may endanger children's physical or psychological well being.

P–5.4—We shall not allow a student to pass a course or move to the next level of the profession if he/she has not demonstrated expected levels of knowledge and competence in course content *or* if he/she does not demonstrate the ability to relate positively and effectively with children and families.

P–5.5—We shall build into all required training minimum required levels of participation and demonstrations of understanding and competence.

P–5.6—When we have made a concerted effort to work with a student, and the student still does not demonstrate the intellectual, physical, or social-emotional capacity to work effectively with children and families, we shall make every effort to counsel the student out of the field.

P–5.7—We shall use the NAEYC Code of Ethical Conduct to assist adult learners in making sound decisions concerning their work with children and families.

6. Ethical responsibilities to community, society, and the field of early childhood education

Early childhood adult educators have extensive knowledge, expertise, and education and often have a profound impact on the field of early childhood education in their communities. Because of this leadership role they have responsibilities to community, society, and the field of early childhood education above and beyond what is expected of those who work in programs serving young children.

Ideals

I–6.1—To train caring and competent teachers who will provide safe and nurturing care and education for young children and be supportive of their families.

I–6.2—To prepare students to work successfully in and to respect the culture of the communities in which they are placed.

I–6.3—To continue to grow and learn and to base practice on the best current knowledge available.

I–6.4—To encourage the developing professionalism of the adult learners with whom we work.

I–6.5—To make other professionals, the public, and policy makers aware of the importance of the early years and the positive impact on society of high-quality early childhood programs staffed by well-trained early childhood professionals.

I–6.6—To strengthen and expand the knowledge base of early childhood education.

I–6.7—To advocate on behalf of children, families, high-quality programs and services for children, and professional development for the early childhood workforce.

I–6.8—To conduct research that reflects the experiences of children from diverse language, racial/ethnic, cultural, and socioeconomic backgrounds.

Principles

P–6.1—We shall be accurate and truthful when we provide recommendations and serve as references for individuals seeking admission to programs, applying for certification, or seeking employment.

P–6.2—In our role as early care and education experts, we shall base recommendations on our informed and unbiased professional opinion. We shall exercise caution before recommending commercial products or services.

P–6.3—When asked to provide an informed opinion on issues/practices, we shall make every effort to support children and families by basing our statements on current child development and early childhood education research.

P–6.4—We shall help adult learners learn to interpret and communicate assessment information in ways that convey the strengths of children and the limitations of the evaluation instruments.

P–6.5—We shall ensure that research we conduct appropriately reflects the diversity of the population upon whom its results may have future impact.

PART II
Building Effective Professional Development Systems

Workforce Designs
A Policy Blueprint for State Early Childhood Professional Development Systems

Early Childhood Education Professional Development
Training, Technical Assistance, and Adult Education Glossary

Using the New NAEYC Professional Preparation Standards

Contents

Sarah LeMoine

Workforce Designs

A Policy Blueprint for State Early Childhood Professional Development Systems

INTRODUCTION

NAEYC formulated this state professional development systems policy blueprint as part of the Early Childhood Workforce Systems Initiative. This initiative focuses on the underlying state public policies that support integrated early childhood professional development systems.

Integrated early childhood professional development system: A comprehensive system of preparation and ongoing development and support for all early childhood education professionals working with and on behalf of young children.

An integrated system crosses sectors serving early education professionals working in direct and nondirect service roles. Such roles may be in Head Start; for-profit and not-for-profit child care programs in centers and homes; state prekindergarten programs in community-based and school-settings; public school programs; early intervention and special education

services; resource and referral agencies; higher education institutions; state departments of education, licensing, health, and other early childhood education related departments.

This blueprint focuses on the policies that connect professional development activities and that support and make possible effective implementation of a state system of professional development. It highlights principles and six policy areas that build or sustain an integrated system—a system that ensures quality in all settings in which early childhood professionals work. These principles and highlighted policy areas look beyond the status quo; they are aimed at the development and retention of a competent and stable early childhood workforce—a skilled cadre of effective, diverse, and adequately compensated professionals.

Principles define fundamental values. In this blueprint the principles for policy making are overarching value statements that are applied in each of the six highlighted policy areas.

Policy provides goals and procedures that guide decisions and actions. Governments, businesses, professions, and other entities develop and employ policies. Public policies, the focus of this blueprint, can be in legislation—articulated in statute, in executive order, or in department regulation. Policies can also be captured via operational documentation that may or may not be referenced in laws or rules.

This policy blueprint also includes a listing of sample state strategies in each of the six key policy areas.

Strategies define the "how"—the plans to do or achieve something, such as implementation of policies.

This policy blueprint was designed for—and with input from—state policy makers, early education advocates, and program administrators working to connect professional development activities and initiatives into an integrated system. The blueprint also was developed with input from other national organizations and experts working to strengthen professional development and career systems for the early childhood workforce. (For additional information about the development of the policy blueprint, see Appendix C, which includes a full listing of both input and feedback participants).

Since state policies do not begin—and will not end up—in the same place, this tool is intended to serve as a starting point for states to expand, change, and adapt for their own political and professional contexts and needs. The blueprint is the first in a series of related resources being developed by the Early Childhood Workforce Systems Initiative. Forthcoming are an executive summary of the blueprint designed specifically for policy makers, online state policy profiles with additional examples or sample language in each policy area, a state needs/gaps analysis tool, and other resources.

Statement of need

The Early Childhood Workforce Systems Initiative comes at a critical time as policy makers place increasing attention on—and accountability for—children's readiness for school. Publicly funded preschool is expanding across the nation. Millions of children, some as young as six weeks, need child care for all or part of a day, week, and year. These children typically receive care and education from multiple sectors of the early childhood system: Head Start, child care programs, public prekindergarten, and other programs.

Research is clear that children who attend high-quality early childhood education programs are more likely to be ready for school and for life. The benefits of all children having access to good early development and learning experiences go beyond the individual child to the society as a whole (Berrueta-Clement et al. 1992; Ramey & Campbell 1999; Reynolds 2000). Research also tells us that qualified and well-compensated professionals are essential to ensuring high-quality early childhood education programs (Phillips 2008). However, the lack of cross-sector systems of professional development for early childhood educators in classrooms and homes, program administration, and other parts of the field creates a serious barrier to providing high-quality education for all young children.

Despite the growing attention to the importance of quality early education, the compensation (wages and benefits) of early childhood educators, particularly in community-based programs, remains untenable. Many individuals working in the field earn very low wages, and few have health care or retirement benefits sponsored by their employers. As a result, early childhood education programs find it extremely difficult to attract and retain highly educated and skilled staff. Additionally, the increased demands at the state and federal levels for higher education credentials without significant linked increases in compensation exacerbate the existing crisis.

Early childhood educators and child outcomes

Many studies point to the knowledge and skills of early childhood program staff as the cornerstone of high quality early childhood education programs. Specialized knowledge and professional development in how young children develop and learn is critical, as is the quality of interactions between program staff and children (Shonkoff & Phillips 2000). Unfortunately, the qualifications of early childhood educators in child care centers and family child care homes is declining and highly qualified professionals are retiring (Herzenberg, Price, & Bradley 2005). Additionally, a recent national survey of early childhood teacher preparation programs in two- and four-year colleges and universities indicates that a majority of early childhood personnel—teachers, administrators, paraeducators, specialists, and others—are not adequately prepared to educate young children with disabilities (Chang, Early, & Winton, 2005).

To ensure quality, there also must be continuity of program staff, which is known to have a positive impact on children's learning (Harms, Cryer, & Clifford 1990; Honig 1993; Lally et al. 1995; Schor 1999; Bergen, Reid, & Torelli 2001). However, the inadequate compensation makes it difficult to attract well-educated individuals to the field, resulting in an annual teacher turnover rate estimated to be at least 30 percent, a rate far exceeding most every other industry in our economy (Bellm & Whitebook 2006).

In addition to practitioners' knowledge and skills, and continuity of relationships, diversity in all arenas of the early childhood education field is necessary to ensure educational equity for all young children. As the demographics of our nation shift and the racial and linguistic diversity of our children increases, it is imperative that teachers and administrators have the skills to work with children and their families to be culturally as well as linguistically and developmentally appropriate. Approximately 45 percent of children younger than 5 are racially, ethnically, or linguistically diverse, and this percentage is expected to grow over the next decade (U.S. Census Bureau 2004). Diversity in early care and education program staff encourages and supports children's positive identity development and prepares them for success in an ever-changing and increasingly diverse society. In the same vein, diversity of early childhood leadership encourages young professionals in aide and beginning teacher roles (NBCDI 1993; Calderón 2005; Ray, Bowman, & Robbins 2006).

Systems of professional development

An effective process of professional development includes a number of criteria. It is important for the growth of all early childhood professionals—at all levels of expertise—to be ongoing.

Professionals need to continue to incorporate new knowledge and skill, through a coherent and systematic program of learning experiences. Those experiences must be grounded in theory and research; be outcomes based; structured to promote linkages between theory and practice; and responsive to each learner's background, experiences, and the current context of his/her role.

Effective learning experiences include a variety of methodologies—the methodology matching the goal of the experience (for example, information dissemination, skill, values clarification). Professional development activities include university/college courses, pre- and inservice training sessions, observation with feedback from a colleague, mentoring, coaching, and other forms of job-related technical assistance. Each learner should participate in planning her/his professional development and work with a supervisor/advisor to develop a plan. Credit-bearing course work is included whenever possible. Professional development providers must have an appropriate knowledge and experience base in early childhood education content as well as in the principles of adult learning (NAEYC 1994, 2005).

Most state early childhood education professional development activities strive to provide effective preparation, development, and supports to address the professional knowledge, stability, and diversity that relate to program quality. However, while many states have components of a professional preparation, development, and career system, many policies and initiatives are not yet linked, and some are nonexistent. The professional standards and requirements for early childhood education staff, for example, vary according to funding streams or program type:

- Most states have no legal requirements for a teacher to have training or education in child development prior to working in a child care center or family child care home.

- The recent reauthorization of the Head Start Act requires that by 2013 all Head Start teachers will have at least an associate's degree and that 50 percent of those teachers will have earned a bachelor's degree in early childhood.

- Many states require teachers in state-funded prekindergarten classrooms to have a bachelor's degree.

- Many states require less early childhood preparation of child care administrators than is required of teachers.

- States typically do not require elementary school administrators to have early childhood education course work.

- While child care licensing regulators/staff are often required to have a bachelor's degree, the mandate may not include any specifications for early childhood education-related coursework or training.

- NAEYC's Early Childhood Associate Degree Accreditation requires faculty to have a graduate degree in early childhood education, child development, or individual-family studies.

Career pathways for early childhood educators are often unclear or not linked across sectors and functions. Many staff participate in professional development seminars and courses that frequently do not lead to a credential or degree. In addition, there is often no articulation between associate degree and baccalaureate degree programs or with credit-bearing community-based training and education opportunities. Further, the costs of professional preparation and professional development put an enormous financial burden on individuals and programs.

Additionally, compensation is low throughout the field and even within a sector there can be large disparities in program reliance on public and private funds. Several important advances in compensation initiatives have been made at the state level, chiefly the T.E.A.C.H.® Early Childhood Project and Child Care Wage$ as well as other state initiatives that provide incentives and rewards linked to an individual attaining higher education credentials, or with such credentials, remaining in the field. However, the base level of compensation—in particular health care and retirement benefits—has not had significant and widespread increases. Early childhood educators with the same credentials can have widely different compensation based on the differing financing levels of different sectors, and programs within those sectors. For example, a preschool teacher with a bachelor's degree and teaching license can be paid thousands of dollars less working in a child care program than a teacher with the same credentials and experience working in a public school setting.

Federal and state policies

Both federal and state policies add to the urgency with which states respond to the professional development needs of the early childhood education workforce:

- Good Start, Grow Smart (GSGS), the early childhood companion to No Child Left Behind, includes an emphasis on providing information and training to parents and early childhood education professionals alike. As part of GSGS, states are to develop voluntary early learning guidelines for young children and related professional development efforts. These efforts often include training on the guidelines and on connecting them with the state's professional standards.

- Head Start's 2007 reauthorization requirements include an interagency State Advisory Council on Early Childhood Education and Care, increased requirements for program staff qualifications and ongoing professional development, and a requirement for each full-time employee to have an individual professional development plan.

- The newly reauthorized Higher Education Opportunity Act includes a new program of grants to states to develop cross-sector, comprehensive professional development systems for early childhood education birth to 5, with loan forgiveness for early childhood educators, and the potential for teacher quality-enhancement partnerships to improve teacher preparation and use the funds on compensation initiatives for early childhood educators who obtain an associate or bachelor's degree.

- At the state policy level, at least 25 states now have bachelor's degree requirements for teachers working in state-financed preschool programs (Barnett et al. 2008).

- As states create quality rating and improvement systems, the higher levels of quality include increased expectations for staff education and credentials.

Integrated professional development system

To effectively meet increasing federal and state mandates and the individual professional and compensatory needs of the early education workforce, states are working to build or increase integrated professional development systems that serve all early childhood education professionals. Previous child care initiatives often play a significant role in supporting integration efforts, sometimes serving as a foundation for cross-sector systems. Such systems provide clear pathways, supports, and compensation for early childhood education professionals. They also connect the entities' financing and their professional preparation and development, both to each other and to the state's overall early childhood system, thus increasing efficiencies and accountability.

NAEYC, through its Early Childhood Workforce Systems Initiative, has a unique and specific focus on essential policy areas that states can use to build, support, and sustain an effective, integrated early childhood education professional development system.

Integrated early childhood professional development system: A comprehensive system of preparation and ongoing development and support for all early childhood education professionals working with and on behalf of young children.

Principles and Essential Policy Areas

State early childhood professional development systems require supportive public policies to ensure that their goals are attainable and successful. The following provides an overview of four principles for policy making and six essential policy areas that make it possible to build and support a comprehensive, integrated professional development system.

These principles and highlighted policy areas look beyond the status quo; they are aimed at the development and retention of the desired, and sustained early childhood workforce—a skilled cadre of effective, diverse, and adequately compensated professionals.

Principles for policy making

Developing policies for integrated early childhood professional development systems is complex and interrelated. As part of this work, state policy makers should reflect on the following questions:

- Does this policy increase integration?

- Does it improve quality?

- Does it support diversity, inclusion, and access?

- Does it increase compensation parity?

Integration; quality assurance; diversity, inclusion, and access; and compensation parity are four principles for policy making that form the cornerstones of this state policy blueprint.

Every time a policy is examined—for development, revision, or any other purpose—there should be reflection on whether these four principles are being addressed. If not, then the examination should include an assessment of why they are not and how policies can be created or revised to incorporate them.

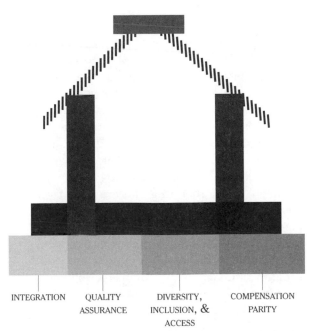

| INTEGRATION | QUALITY ASSURANCE | DIVERSITY, INCLUSION, & ACCESS | COMPENSATION PARITY |

Four Policy-Making Principles

◆ Integration

State policies should create an integrated system of professional development that crosses the early childhood sectors—child care; Head Start; prekindergarten; public schools; early intervention and special education services; and so on. Integrated policies intentionally promote the building and support of an efficient cross-sector system that decreases duplication of efforts and increases sustainability. All related policies need to either be cross-sector or have an element that encourages alignment. When integration and alignment are lacking, there are policy discrepancies and dysfunctions. Policies should be embedded into the early care and education system with appropriate rules, regulations, and statutes in all the agencies that oversee or administer each sector. Policies also should be embedded in other cross-sector activities that touch the workforce. For example, policies may be embedded in or have linkages to the following state implementation strategies:

- quality rating and improvement systems (QRIS),

- unified data systems,

- higher education coordinating bodies or efforts,

- early learning councils, and

- early childhood comprehensive systems planning work.

◆ Quality Assurance

Mechanisms and processes must be in place to ensure accountability for investments in quality professional development that produces positive changes. In addition to fiscal accountability, there should be accountability to the early education professionals, young children and their families, the political system, and the public. Checks and measures should be built into policies that assure quality in professional preparation and development, guarantee that programs are properly implemented, and see that activities are carried out as planned and meet required standards or agreements. Quality assurance processes, including QRIS and iterative evaluations at the individual, program, initiative, and system level, should be built into systems and as they are planned.

Principles define fundamental values. In this blueprint, the principles for policy making are overarching value statements that are applied in each of the six essential policy areas.

◆ Diversity, Inclusion, and Access

Diversity is multidimensional. One part of diversity is the human aspect reflecting the varied demographics of the children, families, and practitioners along the dimensions of age, gender, race, ethnicity, language, ability, sexual orientation, socio-economic status, first and second language development, and so on. Another dimension relates to the structure of the early care and education industry and includes variation by program setting, such as home, center, or school. Funding source and regulatory basis also contribute to diversity. Additionally, the current educational qualifications of the workforce are stratified by gender, race and language. The goal of an integrated professional development system is to encourage diversity but minimize discrepancies in individual and sector access to resources and opportunities, providing equal access to all early education professionals. Access is the how of addressing diversity and inclusion—it includes offering a variety of mechanisms for both information about and the actual professional development activities. All early educators should have access to equitable, high quality professional development.

Attention to diversity, inclusion, and access issues—like those of integration and quality assurance—is a crucial part of all professional development policies. States should create policies that support the recruitment, development, and retention of a workforce that includes professionals who reflect the diversity of the children and families served and that is also prepared to work with children and families of diverse cultures and abilities. These policies should address diversity, inclusion, and access in all early care and education roles: those individuals working directly with children, those preparing and training practitioners, those administering programs, and those advising system and activity implementation.

◆ Compensation Parity

In this blueprint, compensation parity means that compensation is equal or equivalent to other similar fields and that the status of the work and individual's education, experience and responsibilities are recognized and rewarded appropriately. Compensation parity is a principle because it requires focused policy attention. Setting standards for what early childhood educators know and can do must go hand-in-hand with compensation parity, or the field will be unable to compete not only with other education sectors but also with other industries in which workers have comparable credentials but are better compensated.

Essential policy areas

The six essential policy areas of the blueprint are (1) professional standards; (2) career pathways; (3) articulation; (4) advisory structure; (5) data; and (6) financing. None of these policy areas should be addressed in isolation. Similar to the domains of child development, each area relates to and intersects with each other to varying degrees. To be effective, each of these policies must be integrated, attending to all early care and education sectors; include quality assurance mechanisms; and support diversity—each incorporating the cornerstones of the policy-making principles described above. Additionally, each policy must include sufficient and sustainable funding.

Each of the following descriptions includes examples of how the four principles for policy making can be applied in each area, examples of state policy, and various state implementation strategies related to or supported by the policy areas. The examples are meant to illustrate a sample of policy approaches and possible state strategies; they do not represent an exhaustive list. Additional sample policies in each area are being collected and will be available on the Early Childhood Workforce Systems Initiative's Web site at www.naeyc.org/policy/ecwsi/default.asp.

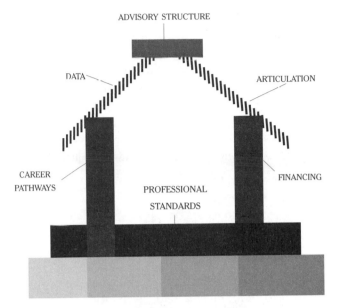

Six Essential Policy Areas

Policy Area 1
Professional Standards

Professional standards define the *what*, or the content, of professional preparation and ongoing development. Most professions require staff to meet both professional preparation and continuing professional development requirements; they require professionals to demonstrate their preparedness to successfully fulfill their job duties and to keep their knowledge and skills up to date. State policies should specify qualifications and ongoing development required for all early care and education professionals—from teacher assistants to trainers and higher education faculty, family child care providers, licensors, resource and referral staff, and program, school, district, and agency administrators. These specifications should address levels and content of education as well as ongoing development. The preparation and ongoing development requirements for these various roles also should be explicitly detailed in career-pathway policies aligning and connecting content.

Applying the principles for policy making

◆ **Integration**: Professional standards for preparation and ongoing development integrate and align existing teacher licensing, state-based credentials, Head Start, prekindergarten, and other related standards.

◆ **Quality Assurance**: Standards meet or incorporate national research-based criteria and are required to be reviewed and updated on a regular basis. Quality assurance mechanisms can set standards for improvement and for quality beyond what is required, and can offer incentives to participate in quality improvement activities.

◆ **Diversity, Inclusion, and Access**: Core professional knowledge/key content areas and standards address diversity and integrate general and special education. Providers, teachers, and other professionals working directly with young children know how to use developmentally appropriate assessment tools. Standards also include a mandatory focus on cultural competence and the process of language acquisition in the content of professional standards.

◆ **Compensation Parity**: Quality rating and improvement systems address staff qualifications and responsibilities, ongoing development, and compensation requirements as part of the system's rating criteria.

State policy examples

The following are two examples (one statutory and one nonstatutory) of states policies related to professional standards. The examples are meant to illustrate various ways states have approached this essential policy area to date and may not address all of the blueprint's overarching policy-making principles.

Statutory example: New Hampshire

New Hampshire Revised Statutes Annotated
Title XII. Public Safety and Welfare
Chapter 170-E. Child Day Care, Residential Care, and Child-Placing Agencies
§ 170-E:50. *Credentialing of Personnel in Early Care and Education Programs; Rulemaking*

I. The commissioner shall adopt rules, under RSA 541-A, relative to accepting applications and issuing a credential to early care and education personnel including, but not limited to child care, preschool, and Head Start program personnel who have requested such a credential and who have satisfied the education and training requirements set forth in the child care program licensing rules established by the department of health and human services. Each application for a credential shall be accompanied by a fee which shall be credited to the general fund. The commissioner shall adopt rules, under RSA 541-A, establishing a fee for this purpose.

Nonstatutory example: Colorado

The Colorado Office of Professional Development's *Colorado Core Knowledge and Standards: A Guide for Early Childhood Professional Development* describes the state's system efforts including the development of "(1) a common core of knowledge and standards; (2) a process for renewing the common core that involves all major stakeholders; (3) a mechanism for bridging non-credit and credit programs; (4) a process for addressing standardization of professional requirements and training; and (5) an early childhood education philosophy that recognizes the diversity of providers, children and families, and the worth of early childhood care and education provided by trained professionals." (Colorado Community College and Occupational Education System et al.1996, 4)

"The areas of core knowledge and standards provide a foundation for common information for agency administrators, instructors, trainers, students, and employees involved in the care and education of young children, and in peripheral occupations. Standards are divided into two levels related to the first two of six levels of credentialing for early childhood professionals. The knowledge and standards are identical for credit and non-credit learning" (Colorado Office of Professional Development 2007, 4).

The 2007 updated version of the guide may be accessed at http://www.netnewsdesk.com/resources/375/File/ECC-OPD/PDF/home/CKSBook.pdf.

Sample implementation strategies

- Credentials, degree programs, and certifications recognized across sectors
- Licensing regulations, departments of education or early childhood, and other agencies requiring state standards specific to age/development and role, regardless of setting

- College and universities' early childhood teacher preparation programs accredited by the National Council for Accreditation of Teacher Education (NCATE) and NAEYC's Early Childhood Associate Degree Accreditation
- Teacher licensure specific to early care and education
- Leadership preparation and development programs include early childhood education content

Policy Area 2
Career Pathways

Professional standards, described in the previous policy area, should align and create coherent career pathways for early childhood professionals. State policy should support continuous progress of individuals. Early childhood professionals need to be able to plan and sequence the achievement of increased qualifications, understand the professional possibilities resulting from such acquisitions, and be appropriately compensated. Policies should institutionalize or embed pathways in all sectors and for all roles—both direct service (those individuals working with young children and their families) and nondirect service (those working on behalf of children and families in training, resource, and other administrative roles). Policies should recognize and support individuals entering the system from other fields and those that move in the early care and education field and among its sectors.

Applying the principles for policy making

◆ **Integration:** Regulatory bodies and quality improvement efforts, such as licensing systems and QRIS, recognize the various roles and levels in the career pathways and encourage increased educational attainment and competency demonstration.

◆ **Quality Assurance:** Career pathway policies include career and academic advisement for participants. Data on professionals' placement and movement on career pathways are verified and assessed.

◆ **Diversity, Inclusion, and Access:** Policies include time requirements for pathways and targeted access supports to gain increasing qualifications.

◆ **Compensation Parity:** Career pathway policies should be aligned with job opportunities that reward investment in professional advancement with salaries comparable to other professions with similar requirements.

State policy examples

The following are two examples of state policy (one statutory and one nonstatutory) related to career pathways. The examples are meant to illustrate various ways states have approached this essential policy area to date and may not address all of the blueprint's overarching policy-making principles.

Statutory example: Connecticut

Connecticut General Statutes Annotated
Title 17B, Social Services
Chapter 319RR. Child Care
§ 17b-733. *Department designated lead agency for child day care services.*

(12) develop and implement, with the assistance of the Child Day Care Council and the Departments of Public Health, Social Services, Education, Higher Education, Children and Families, Economic and Community Development and Consumer Protection, a state-wide coordinated child day care and early childhood education training system (A) for [providers and staff in] child day care centers, group day care homes and family day care homes that provide child day care services, and (B) that makes available to such providers and their staff, within available appropriations, scholarship assistance, career counseling and training, advancement in career ladders, as defined in section 1 of Public Act 03-142, through seamless articulation of levels of training, program accreditation support and other initiatives recommended by the Departments of Social Services, Education and Higher Education.

Nonstatutory example: Pennsylvania

The Pennsylvania Early Learning Keys to Quality Career Lattice outlines eight levels of educational qualifications. The lattice also includes corresponding positions across early childhood sectors of child care/school-age care, Early Head Start/Head Start, early intervention, public school districts, private academic schools, techincal assistance consultants/mentors/trainers, and higher education faculty. As practitioners increase their education, the lattice provides guidance for vertical, horizontal, or diagonal movement across the early education field. The Career Lattice is available online at http://pennaeyc.com/Documents/CareerLattice.pdf.

Sample implementation strategies

• Career ladder or lattice

• Career guide

• Professional development advising

• Continual improvement and/or individual professional development planning

• Mentoring programs/initiatives

• Compensation and rewards

• Pathway information dissemination and tracking via practitioner/workforce registry

• Articulation agreements

Policy Area 3
Articulation

Part of creating a career pathway and building capacity to meet required professional standards involves developing and enforcing policies around articulation. Articulation includes the transfer of professional development participants' credentials, courses, credits, degrees, etc., as well as student performance-based competencies, from one program or institution to another, ideally without a loss of credits. States should require colleges and universities to form articulation agreements that assist early childhood professionals in moving seamlessly through and across undergraduate and graduate degree programs. Grants or specific directions for resource allocations should be attached to such policy requirements; colleges and universities will need fiscal support to change or augment long-standing, institutionalized processes.

Applying the principles for policy making

◆ **Integration:** Qualification requirements for all sectors—Head Start, child care programs, prekindergarten, and others—are supported by articulation policies that connect institutions of higher education to each other and to community-based training.

◆ **Quality Assurance:** Changes are carefully implemented over time, so as not to jeopardize institutional accountability and accreditation.

◆ **Diversity, Inclusion, and Access:** Student counseling/advising is included as part of articulation agreements. Counseling/advising is offered via a variety of methods and in multiple languages as needed.

◆ **Compensation Parity:** Articulation agreements help ensure that financial investments students make in their education result in advancing roles. As institutions create articulation plans, they take into account student financial aid for individuals, release time and substitutes for programs as individuals pursue education and professional development..

State policy examples

The following are two examples of state policy (one statutory and one nonstatutory) related to articulation. The examples are meant to illustrate various ways states have approached this essential policy area to date and may not address all of the blueprint's overarching policy-making principles.

Statutory Example: New Mexico

New Mexico Statutes Annotated
Chapter 21. State and Private Education Institutions
Article 1B. Post-Secondary Education Articulation
§ 21-1B-3. *Articulation plan; development; implementation; establishment of transfer module*

A. The commission shall establish and maintain a comprehensive statewide plan to provide for the articulation of educational programs and facilitate the transfer of students between institutions.

B. In establishing a statewide articulation plan, the commission shall:

(1) establish a common course naming and numbering system for courses identified as substantially equivalent lower-division courses; provided that the commission shall establish an interim mechanism of a statewide equivalency table that uses a universal taxonomy to identify substantially equivalent courses until the common system is in place;

(2) establish a process to identify courses as substantially equivalent. The process shall:

(a) include a procedure for each course whereby faculty members from each segment teaching the academic discipline will reach mutual agreement on the material to be taught and the competencies to be gained;

(b) ensure that the content of each course is comparable across institutions offering that course;

(c) ensure that substantially all the content agreed to among the institutions as the content to be covered by a course is in fact covered in that course and that students successfully completing the course will achieve like competencies with respect to the content covered; and

(d) ensure that the content requirements for each course will be sufficient to prepare students for upper division course work in that field; and

(3) define, publish and maintain modules of lower-division courses accepted for transfer at all institutions and meeting requirements for lower-division requirements established for associate and baccalaureate degree-granting programs.

C. The commission shall ensure that institutions develop transfer modules that include approximately sixty-four hours of lower-division college-level credit.

D. Transfer modules shall include a common general education core component of not less than thirty-five semester hours. This general education core shall include a comprehensive array of lower-division college-level courses designed to demonstrate skills in communication, mathematics, science, social and behavioral science, humanities, fine arts or comparable areas of study coordinated for the purpose of providing a foundation for a liberal education for all programs normally leading to a baccalaureate degree. The general education core shall transfer as a block and count as required lower-division coursework toward a degree, and any course in the core shall be transferable and shall count as credit hours toward fulfilling an institution's general education core requirements.

E. Any course in the general education core may be offered for dual credit to secondary school students and, upon successful completion, the course shall be transferable to any institution and shall count as fulfilling a required lower-division course.

F. A discipline module shall consist of an agreed-upon number of hours and courses, including the general education core, of approximately sixty-four hours applicable to the discipline and any course within the discipline module is transferable and shall count toward fulfilling degree requirements at a four-year institution.

Nonstatutory example: Montana

Montana's Early Childhood Higher Education Consortium guides the development of consistency in course work across higher education programs. Articulation agreements between tribal and community colleges and four year institutions have been established. A 24 credit core in early childhood education is delivered at eight outreach sites and leads to a Child Development Associate (CDA) credential, a college certificate (30 credits), or an associate's or bachelor's degree in early childhood education or a degree with a minor in early childhood education. Some tribal colleges offer core early childhood courses that articulate into the bachelor's degree programs as well. Following the core, students can continue to complete a degree through online options through various colleges. Some courses are taught collaboratively between institutions and offered in an intensive format.

The Early Childhood Project (ECP) at Montana State University sponsors the Early Childhood Higher Education Consortium. Funded by the Montana Department of Public Health and Human Services Early Childhood Services Bureau, ECP facilitates the state's professional development plans and activities with partner organizations across the state. More information about ECP is available online at www.montana.edu/ecp/.

Sample implementation strategies

- Professional development advising and/or course counseling
- Modularized workshops
- Credit for prior learning or credentials
- Articulation of career and technical education/technical preparation into certificate or associate degree programs
- Shared courses and/or faculty
- Program-to-program agreements
- Institution-to-institution agreements
- Common core content or course numbering
- Statewide articulation approach
- Colleges and universities' early childhood teacher preparation programs accredited by the National Council for Accreditation of Teacher Education (NCATE) and NAEYC's Early Childhood Associate Degree Accreditation

Policy Area 4
Advisory Structure

Professional development system coordination does not happen by chance. Effective systems are supported by a policy requiring a specific group of people to focus on this work. State policy should require the creation of an advisory structure to examine needs and provides policy recommendations to the entity or combined entities funding the professional development system. The advisory body should be free standing and have some authority or direct link to authority in the state's governance structure. For this group's work to be recognized and valued across sectors, its composition must include representatives from the diverse settings, auspices, and roles of the early childhood field and professional development system supports. Requiring this makeup sets the context for ensuring cross-sector, integrated recommendations. The work of the advisory structure also should be transparent, taking input and feedback from individuals and other stakeholders. Each sector must respect and be willing to collaborate with other sectors to create an integrated system that does not depend on the different funding streams for different types of programs or families served.

Applying the principles for policy making

◆ **Integration:** Policies ensure the advisory structure includes representatives from all early childhood education sectors. The structure builds off of and expands on the existing work in each sector with a goal of meeting the needs of the workforce in its broadest definition. Previous leadership and efforts are acknowledged and integrated as appropriate.

◆ **Quality Assurance:** The advisory structure engages in strategic planning and regularly reviews the progress of plans and recommendations, making adjustments as needed. The structure is required to gather input from stakeholders/public to inform planning and recommendations.

◆ **Diversity, Inclusion, and Access:** Minimum composition requirements for the advisory body are specified, recognizing the importance of perspectives representing the diversity of the field and leaving space and opportunity for the list of participants to be expanded as needed.

◆ **Compensation Parity:** The advisory body explicitly addresses compensation parity for all levels of roles and responsibilities in programs. Members of the advisory body understand the nexus of compensation and policies that will enhance the quality of the professionals as well as their retention.

State policy examples

The following are two examples of state policy (one statutory and one nonstatutory) related to advisory structures. The examples are meant to illustrate various ways states have approached this essential policy area to date and may not address all of the blueprint's overarching policy-making principles.

Statutory example: Hawaii

Hawaii Revised Statutes Annotated
Laws 2008, 1st Special Session, Act 14
Chapter [undesignated], Early Learning System
(Senate Bill No. 2878)
Section 2, Early Learning System
§ 3. *Early Learning Council*

(a) There is established an early learning council which shall be attached to the department of education for administrative purposes only, notwithstanding any other law to the contrary. To the extent permissible by law, the council shall develop and administer the early learning system established in section 2 to benefit all children throughout the state, from birth until the time they enter kindergarten. In developing the early learning system, the council shall, among other things:...

(8) Coordinate efforts to develop a highly-qualified, stable, and diverse workforce, including:

(a) Ensuring that more early childhood educators and administrators, existing or potential, have opportunities to receive early childhood education degrees, including offering higher education scholarships;

(b) Increasing the availability of early childhood education coursework, including distance learning courses and community-based early childhood education training;

(c) Providing access to continuing professional development for all educators and administrators;

(d) Establishing a system for awarding appropriate credentials to educators and administrators, as incentives to improve the quality of programs and services, relevant to the various early learning approaches, service deliveries, and settings, such as for experience or coursework or degrees completed;

(e) Providing consultation on the social-emotional development of children; and

(f) Providing substitute teacher allowances....

(15) Consult with community groups, including statewide organizations that are involved in early learning professional development, policy and advocacy, and early childhood programs, to broaden the council's knowledge of early learning....

(b) The council shall consist of the following voting members:

(1) The superintendent of education or the superintendent's designee;

(2) The director of human services or the director's designee;

(3) The director of health or the director's designee;

(4) The president of the University of Hawaii or the president's designee;

(5) A representative of center-based program providers;

(6) A representative of family child care program providers;

(7) A representative of family-child interaction learning program providers;

(8) A representative of philanthropic organizations that support early learning; and

(9) Two representatives of the Hawaii Council of Mayors.

The council shall invite the director of the Hawaii head start state collaboration office, the chief executive officer of the Kamehameha Schools, and the executive director of the Hawaii Association of Independent Schools, or their designees, to serve as voting members of the council.

Except for the superintendent of education, directors of state departments, president of the University of Hawaii, director of the Hawaii head start state collaboration office, chief executive officer of the Kamehameha Schools, and executive director of the Hawaii Association of Independent Schools, or their designees, and the two representatives of the Hawaii Council of Mayors, the members shall be nominated and, by and with the advice and consent of the senate, appointed by the governor.

(c) Except for the superintendent of education, directors of state departments, president of the University of Hawaii, director of the Hawaii head start state collaboration office, chief executive officer of the Kamehameha Schools, and executive director of the Hawaii Association of Independent Schools, or their designees, members of the council shall serve staggered terms as follows:

(1) The representative of center-based program providers shall serve a two-year term;

(2) The representative of family child care program providers shall serve a three-year term;

(3) The representative of family-child interaction learning program providers shall serve a three-year term;

(4) The representative of philanthropic organizations that support early learning shall serve a two-year term; and

(5) Of the two representatives of the Hawaii Council of Mayors, one shall serve a two-year

of proposed new requirements, and to help assess the size of the task of training the next generation of workers to care for young children." (Whitebook et al. 2006, 3). California's workforce studies are available online at http://www.irle.berkeley.edu/cscce/2006/california-early-care-and-education-workforce-study/.

Sample implementation strategies

Collection of

- Disaggregated baseline data with periodic updates allowing for measurement of progress

- Demographic data informing needs, gaps, diversity issues, and barriers to access

- Data related to training type and attendance, educational attainment, content focus, and student performance

- Data on the location and disbursement of training and professional development providers and centers and higher education institutions

- Data on the utilization of financial aid

- Data on staff retention, compensation, and turnover rates by reason, areas, roles, and other factors

- Local, state, federal, and private resources financing any part of the professional development system

Policy Area 6
Financing

All systems require funding to operate. Resources have to come with direction. Professional development systems benefit from financing policies that ensure monies are directed where they are most needed and that they are used efficiently. Some degree of specificity must exist to do the needed or newly required work so that funds are not used to backfill gaps. This direction is especially important in a field in which resources are so scarce. State policies should support the financing of integrated professional development systems in four specific areas:

1. **Financial support for early childhood professionals** to obtain education and ongoing development, based on need.

2. **Financial support for programs/workplaces** that facilitate professional development through

resources for release time and substitute staff, teacher mentors and coaches, purchase of materials and equipment, and other supports.

3. **Explicit rewards and compensation parity** for attainment of additional education and development. Other financing mechanisms such as higher reimbursement rates and grants that reflect the cost of quality do not always take into account or sufficiently address the cost of compensation parity.

4. **Financing of the professional development system infrastructure,** which may be linked and/or embedded in the state's larger early childhood system. Infrastructure pieces that require financing may include the advisory body, data systems, support to higher education institutions and training systems, and quality assurance processes.

Applying the principles for policy making

◆ **Integration**: Federal, state, and private sources are coordinated to fund professional development system needs.

◆ **Quality Assurance**: Policies ensure that funders, administrators, participants, and families know what resources are available, where and how they are being directed, and why.

◆ **Diversity, Inclusion, and Access**: Barriers to financial aid and scholarships are examined, and relevant access policies are crafted. Policies also ensure access to ongoing professional development and financing of the governance and institutional aid to higher education and to early childhood programs.

◆ **Compensation Parity**: Policies include specific and adequate financing in all sectors of the system to support compensation equivalent to positions within and across fields requiring similar preparation and experience.

State policy examples

The following are two examples of state policy (one statutory and one nonstatutory) related to financing. The examples are meant to illustrate various ways states have approached this essential policy area to date and may not address all of the blueprint's overarching policy-making principles.

Statutory example: Wyoming

Wyoming Statutes Annotated

Title 14. Children

Chapter 4. Child Care Facilities

Article 2. Quality Child Care

§ 14-4-204. *Educational development scholarships and continuing education grants*

(a) The department by rule and regulation shall provide educational development scholarships to assist the owners or staff of child caring facilities to attain certificates or degrees in early childhood development or a related field. Payments under this subsection shall be conditioned upon the recipient of the educational development scholarship entering into a contract to work for a child caring facility in this state for a period as provided in subsection (d) of this section after receiving the certificate or degree.

(b) A recipient of an educational development scholarship pursuant to this section who breaches the contract required by subsection (a) of this section shall repay that portion of funds provided to the recipient pursuant to this article that is for educational developmental expenses accruing during or after the semester in which the recipient breached the contract, together with attorney fees and costs incurred in collection.

(c) The department by rule and regulation shall provide continuing education grants to child caring facilities to assist the owners or staff of those facilities to obtain continuing education training in early childhood development or related topics. Payments under this subsection shall be conditioned on the following:

> (i) The recipient of the continuing education training provided through the grant entering into a contract to work for a child caring facility in this state for a period as provided in subsection (d) of this section after receiving the training; and
>
> (ii) An in-cash cost sharing contribution of at least ten percent (10%) from the facility employing the staff member at the time of continuing education training.

(d) The department shall set a formula for duration of contractual commitments under this section through rule and regulation. Commitment duration shall be based on the value of the educational opportunity and shall be commensurate with the magnitude of the grant.

(e) A recipient of a continuing education grant pursuant to this section shall repay all funds provided to the recipient pursuant to the grant, together with attorney fees and costs incurred in collection, if the recipient breaches the contract required by subsection (c) of this section.

Nonstatutory example: Ohio

Ohio's overarching goal is a system for delivery of quality early childhood services that includes a comprehensive, coordinated, accessible, and flexible professional development system. Early childhood professionals have access to professional development opportunities and on-going supports that build their knowledge, competencies and skills for working with young children (ages birth–8). The Ohio Early Childhood Professional Development Network drives the state's professional development system activities. Cross-sector professionals comprise the network's leadership team, bringing financing from multiple sectors and sources. System priorities are funded by Build Ohio; the Bureau of Child Care and Development, Ohio Department of Jobs and Family Services; the Head Start state collaboration office; and the Ohio Department of Education.

More information about Ohio's Early Childhood Professional Development Network is available online at www.ohpdnetwork.org.

Sample implementation strategies

- Financial aid such as scholarships, grants, and loan forgiveness
- Paid release time
- Substitute teachers
- Salary scales
- Wage supplements
- Health insurance coverage or reimbursement
- Rewards and bonuses for obtaining degrees or credentials

- Department of Labor and other apprenticeship programs

- Grants to programs to increase credentials and professional development through QRIS

- Performance-based contracting

- Coordination of federal, state, local, and private resources and public/private partnership

Conclusion

Early childhood education professionals need preparation, ongoing development, and support to ensure that our nation's youngest children have quality early learning experiences. In turn, state professional development systems need the support of public policies to offer this essential development. To build and sustain a competent early childhood education workforce, these policies must address all sectors of the field and all service roles—both direct and nondirect—in each sector.

With attention to the policy-making principles of **integration; quality assurance; diversity, inclusion, and access; and compensation parity** NAEYC recommends that states examine and build their public policies in six essential areas:

1. Professional standards

2. Career pathways

3. Articulation

4. Advisory structure

5. Data

6. Financing

States applying the policy-making principles and addressing these essential areas support the infrastructure and goals of integrated professional development systems for early childhood education. Such policies help connect professional development activities and components and support a comprehensive system that serves all early educators—moving our nation closer to a competent early childhood education workforce that can in turn provide the quality learning experiences that all of our nation's young children deserve.

References

Barnett, W., J. Hustedt, A. Friedman, J. Boyd, & P. Ainsworth. 2008. *The state of preschool 2007.* New Brunswick, NJ: National Institute for Early Education Research.

Bellm, D., & M. Whitebook. 2006. *Roots of decline: How government policy has de-educated teachers of young children.* Berkeley, CA: Center for the Study of Child Care Employment.

Bergen, D., R. Reid, & L. Torelli. 2001. *Educating and caring for very young children: The infant/toddler curriculum.* New York: Teachers College Press.

Berrueta-Clement, J., L. Schweinhart, W. Barnett, A. Epstein, & D. Weikart. 1992. *Changed lives: The effects of the Perry Preschool Program on youths through age l9.* Ypsilanti, MI: High/Scope.

Calderón, M. 2005. *Achieving a high-quality preschool teacher corps: A focus on California.* Washington, DC: National Council of La Raza.

Whitebook, M., L. Sakai, F. Kipnis, Y. Lee, D. Bellm, M. Almaraz, & P. Tran. 2006a. *California Early Care and Education Workforce Study: Licensed child care centers. Statewide 2006.* Berkeley, CA: Center for the Study of Child Care Employment, & San Francisco, CA: California Child Care Resource and Referral Network.

Whitebook, M., L. Sakai, F. Kipnis, Y. Lee, D. Bellm, R. Speiglman, M. Almaraz, L. Stubbs, & P. Tran. 2006b. *California Early Care and Education Workforce Study: Licensed family child care providers. Statewide 2006.* Berkeley, CA: Center for the Study of Child Care Employment, & San Francisco: California Child Care Resource and Referral Network.

Chang, F., D. Early, & P. Winton. 2005. Early childhood teacher preparation in special education at 2- and 4-year institutions of higher education. *Journal of Early Intervention* 27 (2): 110–24.

Colorado Community College and Occupational Education System, Colorado Department of Human Services—Office of Child Care Services, Colorado Department of Education, and Colorado Governor's Office. 1996. *Colorado core knowledge and standards: A guide for early childhood professional development.* Colorado: Author.

The Colorado Office of Professional Development. 2007. Colorado core knowledge and standards: A guide for early childhood professional development. http://pennaeyc. com/Documents/CareerLattice.pdf. Colorado: Author.

Harms, T., D. Cryer, & R. Clifford. 1990. *Infant/toddler Environment Rating Scale.* New York: Teachers College Press.

Herzenberg, S., M. Price, & D. Bradley. 2005. *Losing ground in early childhood education: Declining workforce qualifications in an expanding industry,* 1979–2004. Washington, DC: Economic Policy Institute.

Honig, A.S. 1993. Mental health for babies: What do theory and research teach us? *Young Children* 48 (3): 69-76.

Lally, J.R., A. Griffin, E. Fenichel, M. Segal, E. Szanton, & B. Weissbourd. 1995. *Caring for infants and toddlers in groups: Developmentally appropriate practice.* Washington, DC: Zero to Three.

Montana Early Childhood Project. 2003. *A guide to Montana early childhood higher education programs.* Bozeman: Montana State University.

NAEYC. 1994. Conceptual framework for early childhood professional development. Position statement. *Young Children* 49 (3): 68–77.

NAEYC. 2005. Standard 10, topic area 10-E: Personnel policies. In *Early childhood program standards and accreditation criteria: The mark of quality in early childhood education.* Washington, DC: Author.

NBCDI (National Black Child Development Institute). 1993. *Paths to African American leadership positions in early childhood education: Constraints and opportunities.* Washington, DC: Author.

Phillips, D. 2008. *A science-based framework for early childhood policy.* Washington DC: National Scientific Council on the Developing Child.

Ramey, C., & F. Campbell. 1999. *Early learning, later success: The Abecedarian Study.* Birmingham: University of Alabama at Birmingham, Civitan International Research Center.

Ray, A., B. Bowman, & J. Robbins. 2006. *Preparing early childhood teachers to successfully educate all children: The contribution of four-year undergraduate teacher preparation programs.* Chicago: Erikson Institute.

Reynolds, A.J. 2000. *Success in early intervention: The Chicago child-parent centers.* Lincoln: University of Nebraska Press.

Schor, E. 1999. *Early brain development and child care.* New York: Bantam.

Schweinhart, L.J., J. Montie, Z. Xiang, W.S. Barnett, C.R. Belfield, & M. Nores. 2005. Lifetime effects: The High/Scope Perry Preschool Study through age 40. *Monographs of the High/Scope Educational Research Foundation, No. 14.* Ypsilanti, MI: High/Scope.

Shonkoff, J.P., D.A. Phillips, eds., & the Committee on Integrating the Science of Early Childhood Development. 2000. *From neurons to neighborhoods: The science of early childhood development.* Washington, DC: National Academy Press.

U.S. Census Bureau. 2004. *Racial and ethnic composition: Percentage of U.S. children by race and Hispanic origin from interim national population projections for 2008 through 2018.* Washington, DC: Author.

A special thank you is also extended to the following NAEYC staff who provided both input and feedback on this blueprint

- Adele Robinson—Associate Executive Director, Policy and Public Affairs

- Davida McDonald—Senior Public Policy Advisor

- Jerlean Daniel—Deputy Executive Director

- Peter Pizzolongo—Director of Training and Associate Director, Professional Development

- Alison Lutton—Director of Higher Education Accreditation and Program Support

- Gwen Simmons—Director, Affiliate Relations

- Sara Dix—Assistant Director, Affiliate Relations

- Mark Ginsberg—Executive Director

- Kristina Gawrgy—Public Affairs Associate

Appendices

APPENDIX A— About the Early Childhood Workforce Systems Initiative

The National Association for the Education of Young Children's (NAEYC) Early Childhood Workforce Systems Initiative is sponsored by Cornerstones for Kids and the Birth to Five Policy Alliance. (For additional information, please see http://birthtofivepolicy.org.)

The goals of the Early Childhood Workforce Systems Initiative are to

- Formulate a policy blueprint for state early childhood education professional development systems

- Develop an interactive Web interface that provides direct links to states' public policies and key professional development system initiatives and elements as outlined by the state policy blueprint

- Provide national opportunities for collaboration among state policy leaders and administrators, including face-to-face meetings and technology enhanced interactions to create a network of those whose work directly impacts the early childhood workforce

- Collaborate with other organizations and stakeholders working to strengthen the professional preparation and professional development of early childhood educators

- Provide collaboration consultation to pilot states on the policy blueprint and support for such activities.

The efforts of many groups have created a significant depth of expertise in early childhood professional development activities and have helped to move this work forward on national, state, and local levels, impacting early childhood education professionals across the nation. Additionally, various national groups such as the former Wheelock College Center for Career Development, Head Start, the National Child Care Information Center, the National Professional Development Center on Inclusion, and others provided professional development system frameworks and models. The specific policy focus and cross-sector nature of NAEYC's Early Childhood Workforce Systems Initiative provide a different yet complimentary impetus to this work. Using NAEYC's position in the field, this project will assist states in advancing the policy agenda toward building and sustaining a stable, highly skilled, knowledgeable, diverse, and well-compensated professional workforce—the desired early childhood education workforce.

Steering Committee

A five-member Steering Committee provides guidance on the activities of this project:

1. **Anne Mitchell,** Chair—Former President of NAEYC, early childhood policy expert and consultant, and co-founder of the Alliance on Early Childhood Finance.

2. **Linda Espinosa**—Senior Faculty Member at the University of Missouri- Columbia who has studied the early childhood workforce with particular attention to programs, services, and professional training issues concerning children of Latina heritage.

3. **Jacqueline Jones**—Assistant Commissioner of the Division of Early Childhood Education in the New Jersey Department of Education with primary responsibility for early childhood education programs in the state.

4. **Tonya Russell**—Director of the Division of Child Care and Early Childhood Education at the Arkansas Department of Human Services administering the state's Child Care and Development Block Grant.

5. **Marcy Whitebook**—Director of the Center for the Study of Child Care Employment, at the University of California at Berkeley, who has studied and written extensively about the early childhood workforce and associated public policy issues.

APPENDIX B—
Alignment with NAEYC Priorities, Goals, and Work

Founded in 1926, NAEYC is dedicated to issues affecting the education and development of young children, and our more than 80,000 members represent the diversity of the early childhood field. Historically, the Association's mission has been to improve the quality of care and education provided to young children in the United States. This mission includes working to improve professional practice and working conditions in early childhood education. Position statements, standards, and accreditation systems that support the preparation and ongoing development of the early childhood workforce are just some of NAEYC's activities in this area.

▶ Position and Summary Statements

NAEYC's statements, A Conceptual Framework for Professional Development of Early Childhood Educators and Where We Stand on Standards for Programs to Prepare Early Childhood Professionals, are widely used by policy makers, higher education institutions, and advocates.

▶ Conferences and Materials

NAEYC's Annual Conference and Institute on Early Childhood Professional Development provide opportunities to disseminate information and convene all segments of the workforce around key issues of the field. In addition, NAEYC is one of the nation's largest publishers of materials designed for teachers of young children and one of the largest providers of continuing professional education in the field.

▶ Affiliates

NAEYC enjoys a vibrant network of 50 State Affiliates that work to increase understanding and support for high-quality early childhood education among policy makers and the public through a wide range of professional development conferences, advocacy, and public awareness activities. State Affiliates are committed to leadership development by creating opportunities for members to serve on local and state boards, task forces and committees that impact the early childhood field.

▶ Accreditation Systems

For more than 23 years, NAEYC's early childhood center- and school-based program accreditation has set important criteria for professional standards, including 10 accreditation standards for teachers. The Association, in collaboration with the National Council for the Accreditation of Teacher Education (NCATE), has developed national accreditation standards for undergraduate and graduate degrees in early childhood education. NAEYC also recently formulated accreditation standards for associate degree programs in the field and administer the only such national accreditation system.

With this blueprint and related resources, NAEYC provides the field with specific policy areas, goals, and a tool to assess the system-level connectors—including infrastructure and policies—needed to support a comprehensive, integrated early childhood professional development system. The Early Childhood Workforce Systems Initiative, and specifically the development of this state policy blueprint, continues the Association's rich history of professional preparation and development work.

APPENDIX C—
Input and Feedback Processes

Before this state policy blueprint was drafted, more than 50 individuals provided input on key policies they believe are needed to support state integrated early childhood education professional development systems. Participants provided insights through one-on-one interviews or focus groups.

In addition to the Steering Committee's careful review, several focus groups provided feedback on the draft blueprint. A multistate focus group was held at the 8th Annual T.E.A.C.H.® Early Childhood and Child Care WAGE$® National Conference; three focus groups were conducted in Arkansas; and an additional focus group was held in New Jersey. Feedback was also provided on a final discussion draft by state leadership teams participating in Linking Sectors, Advancing Systems: the 2nd Annual State Professional Development Leadership Team Work Day, a pre-Institute session at NAEYC's 2008 Institute for Early Childhood Professional Development, and by members of the Birth to Five Policy Alliance.

NAEYC would like to thank all of the individuals involved in the input and feedback processes for generously sharing their time and expertise.

Input Participants

Individual interview participants

- Nancy Alexander—Executive Director, Northwestern State University Child and Family Network, Louisiana

- Diane Aillet—Career Development Coordinator, Louisiana Pathways

- Donna Alliston—Professional Development Coordinator, Division of Child Care and Early Childhood Education, Arkansas Department of Human Services

- Cecelia Alvarado—Early Childhood Education Consultant and Faculty, Graduate School of Education, George Mason University, Virginia

- Peggy Ball—State Technical Assistance Specialist, National Child Care Information and Technical Assistance Center (NCCIC), and Independent Consultant

- Paula Jorde Bloom—McCormick Tribune Center for Early Childhood Leadership, National-Louis University, Illinois

- Lindy Buch—Director, Office of Early Childhood Education and Family Services, Michigan Department of Education

- Margot Chappel—Director, Nevada Head Start State Collaboration Office

- Judy Collins—Senior Content Specialist, Tribal Child Care Technical Assistance Center (Tri-TAC) and Independent Consultant

- Gayle Cunninghnam—NAEYC* Governing Board and Executive Director, Jefferson County Committee for Economic Opportunity, Alabama

- Judy Fifield—Program Manager, Office of Child Development, New Mexico Children, Youth and Families Department

- Nancy Freeman—Associate Professor of Early Childhood Education, University of South Carolina and President-elect of the National Association of Early Childhood Educators (NAECTE)

- Phoebe Gillespie—Project Director, National Center for Special Education Personnel and Related Service Providers, National Association of State Directors of Special Education (NASDSE)

- Donna Gollnick—Senior Vice President, National Council for Accreditation of Teacher Education (NCATE)

- Carol Hall—Director, Early Childhood School Special Education Staff Development and School Improvement, Educational Service District 112, Washington

- Cindy Harrington—Program Director, Distance Early Childhood Education AA Education Program, University of Alaska

- Kristen Kerr—Executive Director, New York State Association for the Education of Young Children

- Susan Landry—Michael Matthew Knight Professor of Pediatrics, Director, Children's Learning Institute, University of Texas

- Jim Lesko—Education Associate, Early Childhood Education/IDEA Section 619 Coordinator, Delaware Department of Education

- Joan Lessen-Firestone—NAEYC* Governing Board and Director, Early Childhood, Oakland Schools, Michigan

- Catherine Doyle Lyons—Executive Director, Lynn Bennett Early Childhood Education Center, University of Nevada Las Vegas/ Consolidated Students of the University of Nevada Preschool, Preschool Faculty Coordinator and Assistant Professor in residence, Nevada Department of Special Education

- Karen Mason—Executive Director, Idaho Association for the Education of Young Children

- Robin McCants— Early Childhood Specialist, South Carolina Department of Education, Office of Academic Standards: Early Childhood

- Gwen Morgan—Senior Fellow in Early Care and Education Policy, Wheelock College, Massachusetts

- Gail Nourse—Director, Pennsylvania Key

- Patti Oya—Social Services Program Specialist, Early Care and Education Office, Division of Welfare and Supportive Services, Nevada Department of Health and Human Services

- Kris Perry—Executive Director, First 5 California

- Carol Prentice—Program Manager, Alaska System for Early Education Development (Alaska SEED)

- Tom Rendon—Coordinator, Iowa Head Start State Collaboration Office and Iowa Even Start

- Linda Rorman—Head Start-State Collaboration Administrator, Children and Family Services Division, North Dakota Department of Human Services

- Sue Russell—President, NAEYC* and President of Child Care Services Association, North Carolina

- Barb Sawyer—Director of Special Projects, National Association for Family Child Care (NAFCC)

- Lisa Stein—Assistant Professor Atlantic Cape Community College, New Jersey and President, ACCESS – American Associate Degree Early Childhood Educators

- Kathleen Stiles—Executive Director, Smart Start Colorado Office of Professional Development

- Louise Stoney—Co-founder, Alliance for Early Childhood Finance and Independent Consultant, Stoney Associates

- Teri Talan—Assistant Professor, Department of Early Childhood Education, National-Louis University and Director of Research and Public Policy for the Center for Early Childhood Leadership

- Anne Wharff—Program Manager, Child Care Professional Development, Bureau of Child Care and Development, Illinois Department of Human Services

- Sue Williamson—President, National Association for Family Child Care

National DC-area-based focus group participants

- Sarah Daily—Senior Policy Analyst, National Governors Association (NGA)*

- Carol Brunson Day—President, National Black Child Development Institute (NBCDI)

- Lynn Jones—Senior Policy Analyst, ZERO TO THREE*

- Eric Karolak—Executive Director, Early Care and Education Consortium (ECEC)

- Susan Perry Manning—Chief of Programs, National Association of Child Care Resource and Referral Agencies (NACCRRA)

- Jana Martella—Executive Director, National Association of Early Childhood Specialists in State Departments of Education (NAECS/SDE)

- Debbie Moore—Director of Public Policy, NAFCC

- Katherine Beh Neas—Senior Director, Federal and State Government Relations, Easter Seals

- Mary Beth Salomone—Policy Director, ECEC

- Yvette Sanchez—Executive Director, National Migrant and Seasonal Head Start Association (NMSHSA)

- Karen Schulman—Senior Policy Analyst, National Women's Law Center (NWLC)

- Rachel Schumacher—Senior Fellow, Child Care and Early Education Policy, Center for Law and Social Policy (CLASP)*

- Vilma Williams—Director of Training Services, Council for Professional Recognition

- Marty Zaslow—Senior Scholar and Senior Program Area Director for Early Childhood, Vice President for Research, Child Trends

Feedback Participants

Multistate focus group participants

- Autumn Gehri—T.E.A.C.H.® Program Director, Wisconsin Early Childhood Association

- Laurie Litz—Vice President of Workforce Development and Director, T.E.A.C.H.® Early Childhood Pennsylvania

- Edith Locke—Vice President, Professional Development Initiatives Division, Child Care Services Association

- Barb Merrill—Executive Director, Iowa Association for the Education of Young Children and Program Manager, T.E.A.C.H.® Early Childhood IOWA

- Jeanette Paulson—Director of Workforce Initiatives, Wisconsin Early Childhood Association (WECA)

- Jeremy Rueter—T.E.A.C.H.® Program Director, Michigan 4C

- Julie Rogers—Director, T.E.A.C.H.® Early Childhood TA/QA Center, CCSA

- Lori Stegmeyer—Director of Workforce Initiatives, Children's Forum, Inc., Florida

Arkansas focus group participants

- Donna Alliston—Professional Development Coordinator, Division of Child Care and Early Childhood Education, Department of Human Services

- Vernoice Baldwin—Director, University of Arkansas Infant Development Center and University of Arkansas Nursery School

- Marietta Baltz—CCOT Training Advisor, Early Care and Education Projects, University of Arkansas

- Jo Battle—Coordinator, ACQUIRE, Childhood Services, Arkansas State University

- Bobbie Biggs—Professor, College of Education and Health Professions University of Arkansas

- Pam Cicirello—Dean, Allied Heath Early Childhood, Pulaski Technical College

- Mardi Crandall—Instructor, Human Development and Family Studies, University of Arkansas

- Elaine Davis—Director, Resource and Referral, Parents As Teachers

- Judy Eddington—Training Consultant, Division of Developmental Disabilities Services, Department of Human Services

- Joanna Grymes—Associate Professor Early Childhood Education, Arkansas State University

- Michelle Harvey—Registry Coordinator, Arkansas State University Childhood Service

- Shelli Henehan—Director, Preschool Early Childhood, College of Education, University of Arkansas, Fort Smith

- Deniece Honeycutt—Research Associate, College of Education and Health Professions, University of Arkansas

- Phyllis Jackson—Ouachita Technical College Malvern

- Calvin Johnson—Dean, School of Education, University of Arkansas at Pine Bluff

- Traci Johnston—Child Care Program Associate, Cooperative Extension Service, University of Arkansas

- Marsha Jones—Assistant Superintendent of Curriculum and K-5 Instruction, Springdale Schools

- Kathy MacKay—Licensing Coordinator, Division of Child Care and Early Childhood Education, Department of Human Services

- Kim Parsley—Child Care Connections

- Ann Patterson—Director, Arkansas Head Start Collaboration Office

- Brenda Reynolds—Director, Partners/ Welcome the Children

- Linda Rushing—Vice Chancellor, University of Arkansas Monticello, College of Technology-Crossett

- Tonya Russell—Director, Division of Child Care and Early Childhood Education, Department of Human Services

- Susan Slaughter—Pre K SEL, Training Advisor, Early Care and Education Projects, University of Arkansas

- Kathy Stegall—Program Support Administrator, Division of Child Care and Early Childhood Education, Department of Human Services

- Michele Taylor—Child Care Connections
- Carolene Thornton—Director, Center for Effective Parenting
- Nancy vonBargen—State Technical Assistance Specialist for the Administration for Children and Families Region VI, National Child Care Information and Technical Assistance Center
- Julie Williams—Early Childhood Development Program Coordinator, Pulaski Technical College
- NeCol Wilson—Training Advisor, Early Care and Education Projects, University of Arkansas

New Jersey focus group participants

- Lorraine Cooke—Public Policy Chair, New Jersey Association for the Education of Young Children
- Ellen Frede—Co-Director, National Institute for Early Education Research
- Shonda Laurel—Department of Human Services
- Mary Manning-Falzarano—Clearinghouse Manager, Professional Impact NJ
- Holly Seplocha—Associate Professor, Early Childhood Education, William Paterson University
- Beverly Wellons—State Child Care Administrator, Department of Human Services
- Renee Whelan—Professional Development Coordinator, Division of Early Childhood Education, New Jersey Department of Education

States represented at NAEYC's 2008 professional development leadership team work day

- Alabama
- Alaska
- California
- Connecticut
- District of Columbia
- Florida
- Georgia
- Hawaii
- Idaho
- Illinois
- Iowa
- Kansas
- Louisiana
- Massachusetts

National and state organization participants

- Linda Adams—Executive Director, Colorado AEYC
- Agda Burchard—Executive Director, Washington AEYC
- Joan Lombardi—The Children's Project,* Washington, DC
- Gwen Morgan—Senior Fellow in Early Care and Education Policy, Wheelock College, Massachusetts
- Katherine Murphy—Executive Director, Hawaii AEYC
- Sue Russell—President, NAEYC* and President of Child Care Services Association, North Carolina
- Cathy Grace—Professor and Director, National Center for Rural Early Childhood Learning Initiatives, Early Childhood Institute, Mississippi State University
- Libby Hancock—Director, Early Childhood Project, Montana State University
- Elizabeth Shores—Associate Director for Research, Communications, and National Initiatives, Early Childhood Institute, Mississippi State University
- Helene Stebbins—Project Director, National Center for Children in Poverty*
- Kimberly Tice-Colopy—Executive Director, Ohio AEYC
- Margie Wallen—Early Learning Project Manager, Ounce of Prevention Fund*
- Pam Winton— Senior Scientist and Director of Outreach, FPG Child Development Institute and Research Professor, School of Education, University of North Carolina – Chapel Hill, and National Professional Development Center on Inclusion

Contents

Early Childhood Education Professional Development

Training, Technical Assistance, and Adult Education Glossary

A multi-part project of the National Association for the Education of Young Children (NAEYC), the National Association of Child Care Resource and Referral Agencies (NACCRRA), and the Alliance of Early Childhood Teacher Educators (a collaborative effort of the National Association of Early Childhood Teacher Educators [NAECTE] and Associate Degree Early Childhood Teacher Educators [ACCESS])

Professional preparation and ongoing professional development (PD) for the early childhood education workforce is essential to providing high-quality services to children and families. Consistent terminology and definitions related to PD methods, roles, knowledge, and capabilities have emerged as a critical issue for the early education field. Recently, states have experienced new early childhood education system challenges and needs related to training, technical assistance (TA), and adult education. The urgency of these issues grows, particularly as states increase their focus and work on quality improvement activities, including quality rating and improvement systems (QRIS). For example, many states are working to define what training and TA is needed to support successful participation in QRIS, and how it integrates with PD activities and systems; how to determine who can provide training and TA—and how; and how to track and count TA as part of an individual's professional development.

To support related efforts, the National Association for the Education of Young Children (NAEYC) and the National Association of Child Care Resource and Referral Agencies(NACCRRA) jointly developed the glossary of professional development, training, and technical assistance (TA) terms. NAEYC and the Alliance of Early Childhood Teacher Educators (a collaborative effort of the National Association of Early Childhood Teacher Educators and ACCESS–Associate Degree Early Childhood Teacher Educators) jointly developed national education-related definitions.[1]

---

[1]Details about the development process of the training and TA glossary appear in Appendix B.

This glossary is composed of global definitions that embrace what NAEYC and its partners believe define the current best-practice ideals for training, TA and adult education. The definitions were developed for those who provide PD, state policy makers, early education advocates, and program administrators working to connect PD activities and initiatives into an integrated system. NAEYC, NACCRRA and the Alliance hope the definitions will provide a guide for states to adapt and adjust as needed to meet their specific needs in clarifying roles and policies, assist with the related work of determining and supporting the knowledge and capabilities of those providing PD, and also aid in data efforts to count and track all types of PD. We also hope these definitions will help provide common understandings, or starting points, for research and national or cross-state discussions—knowing that there are a variety of different models and approaches to each strategy included in this high-level definitions document.

Although one method of PD delivery is generally predominant in a given situation, these strategies frequently overlap. In fact, best practices in professional development delivery include the use of multiple methods. However, in this glossary, training, TA, and adult education methods are defined as discrete processes. This glossary begins with definitions that provide a broad overview of PD context. The resource then defines specific PD methods of training and TA—including mentoring, coaching, consultation, advising, and peer-to-peer TA. Two appendices also are included in this resource: Appendix A—Technical Assistance Strategies and Implications for Postsecondary Programs and Appendix B—Project Overview and Process.

The job titles of the individuals who provide PD are many and varied—higher education faculty, trainers, program administrators (in their training and TA roles), individual consultants, child care resource and referral training and TA staff, and others. These professionals provide education, training, and/or TA to individuals working or preparing to work with young children and their families and those working or preparing to work on behalf of children in training, licensing, resource, and other administrative roles related to early childhood education. While NAEYC, NACCRRA, and the Alliance of Early Childhood Teacher Educators believe that those who provide PD should possess a high level of knowledge and skills and participate in ongoing professional development, this glossary does not define the core knowledge and capabilities expected of these professionals. In future work, NAEYC, NACCRRA, and the Alliance of Early Childhood Teacher Educators will explore the core knowledge and capabilities of those who provide professional development and what national resources may be helpful to support related state efforts.

Contextual Definitions

The Early Childhood Education Workforce includes those working with young children (infants, toddlers, preschoolers, and school-age children in centers, homes, and schools) and their families or on their behalf (in agencies, organizations, institutions of higher education, etc.), with a primary mission of supporting children's development and learning.

Early Childhood Education Professional Development is a continuum of learning and support activities designed to prepare individuals for work with and on behalf of young children and their families, as well as ongoing experiences to enhance this work. These opportunities lead to improvements in the knowledge, skills, practices, and dispositions of early education professionals. Professional development encompasses *education, training, and technical assistance.*

Some of the early childhood workforce have college degrees in early education, some have degrees in closely related fields, some are enrolled in degree programs, some are taking college courses, some are graduates of technical high schools or technical school programs, some have no previous related education—and almost all of them are engaged in training every year. An individual may engage in all types of PD (education, training, and TA) over the course of a career. Professional development helps early childhood professionals in all roles progress along diverse career pathways that build and reward increasing knowledge and skills.

All professional development (education, training, and TA) should

- be designed using evidence-based best practices[2]; consistent with the principles of adult learning; and structured to promote linkages between research, theory, and practice.

- address the continuum of young children's abilities and needs.

- respond to each learner's background (including cultural, linguistic, and ability), experiences, and the current context of her role and professional goals.

- include resources to ensure access for all.

Individual Professional Development Plans (IPDPs) are documents that provide a framework connecting various professional development experiences to each other and to the common core of knowledge and professional standards for early education professionals. Individual professional development plans are designed to create a holistic approach to building an early childhood professional's capacities and to ensure that individuals remain current regarding knowledge and practices in the field. Individual professional development plans promote professional advancement. They can address career opportunities for those with a goal of pursuing different roles or positions in the field. Individual professional development plans require and support individuals taking responsibility for mapping their own professional development and career pathway.

- Individual professional development plans can be developed in one of two ways:
  - — at the workplace level with review and approval by a supervisor, based on needs and strengths of the individual as identified through self-reflection, performance appraisal, and other information, including program evaluation and improvement processes[3]; and
  - — at the individual level with guidance from an advisor, consultant, mentor, or other TA provider, with a focus on mapping one's own professional development and career pathway.
- Individuals use their IPDPs on an ongoing basis to remain focused on their professional goals and needs.
- IPDPs are reviewed and revised as necessary on at least an annual basis, or as professional goals, development needs, or PD resources or opportunities change.
  - —Individuals review their plans as they reflect on their knowledge, practice, professional development endeavors, and goals—with guidance from an advisor or other TA provider, adult educator, and/or the administrative leadership of the individual's workplace.

All early childhood education professionals should have IPDPs to assist in developing or articulating their career goals, and to guide and inform desired career advancement and decisions regarding PD opportunities.

Training Definitions

Training is a learning experience, or series of experiences, specific to an area of inquiry and related set of skills or dispositions, delivered by a professional(s) with subject matter and adult learning knowledge and skills. A planned sequence of training sessions comprises a training program.

Additional Characteristics of Training

Focus

- Part of professional development that builds or enhances the knowledge and competencies of early childhood education professionals.
- Training sessions and programs can focus on information dissemination; comprehension of content; application of knowledge or skills, and related attitudes and dispositions; analysis or synthesis of content; or a combination of these.

Relationships

- All training is strengthened by trusting and respectful interactions. Participants value each other as resources for learning, in addition to the trainer serving in the official leadership role.
- Because training programs include multiple sessions, they benefit from intentional building of positive relationships between and among trainer(s) and participants.
- Delivered by an individual or a team, to an individual or a group.

Process

- Planned and conducted based on the standards of the profession and an assessment of individual, group, and/or system needs. Standards, needs assessment, and other evidence are also used to define learning outcomes for training session(s).
- Follows adult learning principles including interactive learning activities, exercises, and instructional aides (handouts, audiovisuals, and other components of instruction) to teach the content that supports the defined outcomes.
- Includes an evaluative component that gauges the effectiveness of the training session/program including the resulting increase in participants' knowledge or capabilities.
- Completion of training programs can lead to participants' assessment for award of the Child Development Associate (CDA) Credential or another type of credential, continuing education units (CEUs), clock hours, or certification. In some instances participants who successfully complete a training program are awarded credit hours or may qualify for college credits. Trainers and/or their training content may need to meet specific approval requirements in order for participants to be awarded CEUs, clock hours, or other state-required documentation.
- Should be embedded in the recipient's broader professional development plan.

Duration

- Can occur one time or in a series of sessions (training program).

Delivery

- May be delivered through face-to-face, distance, technology-based, or hybrid methods.

Preservice or *initial training* refers to PD in which an individual engages prior to beginning a position. Preservice training may be required for early childhood professionals to serve in a role.

Professionals engaged in initial training should work alongside or under the supervision of a qualified coworker until such training is completed.

In-service or *ongoing training* is PD in which early childhood professionals engage to enhance their skills and remain current regarding knowledge and practice in the field. In-service training may be required for early childhood professionals to continue serving in a role.

Because of the field's varying requirements, there is often crossover regarding preservice and in-service education and training. An individual could receive preservice education and/or training to be a teaching staff member in a communitybased organization and also receive in-service education and/or training during her employment. The same individual could be pursuing a degree for a role as a teacher in a setting where individual licensure is required (e.g., public schools)— this education would be considered in-service professional development for the individual's current role and would be considered preservice preparation for the certified teaching position. Therefore, the labels preservice and in-service must be seen as related to the requirements of a position or established role in the field.

Technical Assistance Definitions

Technical Assistance (TA) is the provision of targeted and customized supports by a professional(s) with subject matter and adult learning knowledge and skills to develop or strengthen processes, knowledge application, or implementation of services by recipients.

Additional Characteristics of Technical Assistance

Focus

- Supports the reflective processes that professionals need to translate the theories and information learned through education and/or training into best practices.
- Mentoring, coaching, consultation, PD advising, and peer-to-peer TA (defined below) are strategies that may be discrete processes or used as part of education and/or training programs.
- Should be embedded in the recipient's broader professional development plan.

Relationships

- Most TA methods are relationship-based; they benefit from the building of positive, trusting, and respectful relationships.
- May be delivered by an individual or a team, to one individual or a group.

Process

- May include combinations of information and resource dissemination and referrals, coaching, mentoring, consultation, and professional development advising, peer-to-peer TA, as well as other forms of support.

Duration

- Levels, intensity, and duration vary greatly, depending on needs, responses, and resources.

Delivery

- May be provided face-to-face or through distance, technology-based, or hybrid methods.

Mentoring is a relationship-based process between colleagues in similar professional roles, with a more-experienced individual with adult learning knowledge and skills, the mentor, providing guidance and example to the less-experienced protégé or mentee. Mentoring is intended to increase an individual's personal or professional capacity, resulting in greater professional effectiveness.

Additional Characteristics of Mentoring

Focus	• Addresses a specific topic or the protégé's holistic professional growth. • Supports the reflective processes professionals need to translate the theories and information learned through education and/or training into best practices. • Should be included in the recipient's broader professional development plan.
Relationships	• Includes the mentor and protégé establishing and maintaining a positive, trusting, and respectful relationship. • Ideal match up of mentor and protégé is mutually agreed upon rather than assigned. A person may also enlist a mentor, be assigned to a mentor, or the mentor may be assigned to an individual. • Can be accomplished by some supervisors, but should be distinguished from supervisory processes. Should not be used as a method of evaluating job performance.
Process	• Begins with establishing role clarity and goal setting. • Includes the facilitation of adult learning techniques such as guided self-reflection, resulting in the application of new ideas to the protégé's professional practice or personal disposition. • May include unplanned contacts between mentor and protégé when the protégé has questions or specific concerns. • Remains ongoing or concludes by mutual consent or when the protégé has achieved her goals.
Duration	• Ongoing, iterative process.
Delivery	• May be provided face-to-face or through distance, technology-based, or hybrid methods.

Coaching is a relationship-based process led by an expert with specialized and adult learning knowledge and skills, who often serves in a different professional role than the recipient(s). Coaching is designed to build capacity for specific professional dispositions, skills, and behaviors and is focused on goal-setting and achievement for an individual or group.

Additional Characteristics of Coaching

Focus
- Supports the development of specific skills and practices; it is focused on a performance-based outcome(s).
- Should be embedded in the recipient's broader professional development plan that provides the theoretical foundations related to the specific skills being addressed.

Relationships
- Requires interactions that build trust and respect.
- A person may select a coach, be assigned to a coach, or the coach may be assigned to an individual or group.
- Should be distinguished from supervisory processes; however, its findings and conclusions may contribute to job performance evaluation. In these instances, the recipient of the coaching should be made aware of this possibility.

Process
- Begins with a collaborative agreement between the coach and the individual to set the guidelines and goals.
- Includes various combinations of questioning, listening, observation, reflection, feedback, prompting, modeling, and practice.
- Likely to occur through planned onsite contacts.
- Concludes when the specified goal has been achieved.

Duration
- Can occur one time or in a series of sessions, dependent upon the successful achievement of the goal.

Delivery
- May be provided face-to-face or through distance, technology-based, or hybrid methods.

Consultation is a collaborative, problem-solving process between an external consultant with specific expertise and adult learning knowledge and skills and an individual or group from one program or organization. Consultation facilitates the assessment and resolution of an issue-specific concern—a program-/organizational-, staff-, or child-/family-related issue—or addresses a specific topic.

Additional Characteristics of Consultation

Focus

- Resolution of a specific concern or set of concerns.
- Capacity-building approach to facilitate the recipient's continued use of the process employed during or as a result of the consultation.

Relationships

- Requires a collaborative relationship between the consultant and the person to whom he/she provides recommendations.
- Consultants may be engaged by the administrative leadership of a workplace. In some instances the consultancy is arranged or directed by a regulatory or funding agency or organization.

Process

- Begins with the joint development of goals.
- Supports the development of goal-related solutions and the implementation strategies recommended to achieve them. Recommendations may include the provisions of other relationship-based TA methods.
- Likely to occur through planned onsite contacts.
- Concludes with a summary process and an evaluation of the effectiveness of the consultation provided.

Duration

- Generally short term. Long-term relationships with consultants may develop if individuals, programs, or organizations use them for assistance in addressing multiple, often interrelated, concerns over time. As an example, long-term relationships with consultants may evolve as they help guide overall program quality improvement processes.

Delivery

- May be provided face-to-face (onsite or offsite) or through distance, technology-based, or hybrid methods.

Professional Development Advising (sometimes referred to as career or PD counseling) is a one-on-one process through which an advisor offers information, guidance, and advice to an individual about professional growth, career options, and pathways to obtain or meet required qualifications.

Additional Characteristics of PD Advising

Focus

- Supports individuals seeking to further their professional growth and advancement.

Relationships

- Requires establishing and maintaining a trusting and respectful relationship.
- Advisors may be enlisted by an individual or assigned by a system, program, or supervisor.
- Supervision processes may include advising on professional development needs, requirements, and opportunities as an ongoing process and/or as a part of job performance evaluations.

Process

- Begins with career or PD goal setting.
- Includes navigation of resources (financial, educational, and personal) and systems. May include assessment of current educational attainment and the development of an individual professional development plan, offering assistance to recipients in connecting previously taken and potential PD opportunities to achieve the individual's career goals.
- Concludes by mutual consent, when career or other identified goals have been achieved, or may continue throughout a career.

Duration

- May be an ongoing or limited-time process depending on needs, response, and available resources.

Delivery

- May be provided face-to-face (onsite or offsite) or through distance, technology-based, or hybrid methods.

Peer-to-peer TA fosters the development of relationship-based learning and support communities among colleagues, often in like roles. Peer-to-peer TA is based on the premise that a significant expert knowledge base exists in the field and that peers who have solved challenges on the ground have developed tools and strategies that can be shared with their colleagues.

Additional Characteristics of Peer-to-Peer TA

Focus

- Enhancing and encouraging the sharing of information and support between and among interested peers and establishing linkages between individuals invested in professional growth.
- When peer-to-peer TA occurs between two people, it is often called "peer learning." Regular and structured group peer-to-peer TA may be called "Communities of Practice" or "Professional Learning Communities."

Relationships

- Requires respectful and trusting relationships between and among peers.
- May use a combination of formats such as one-to-one, one-to-many, or group-togroup exchanges.
- An essential characteristic of peer-to-peer TA is that participants are on equal footing; supervisors do not participate in peer-to-peer TA with their employees, although they can be called upon to provide information, resources, or other support.

Process

- Peers come together around a shared interest, challenge, or goal. Those engaged in peer-to-peer TA begin their work with a common awareness of the field's challenges and realities. They draw upon many of the same experiences and "speak the same language."
- Each participant offers unique strengths, knowledge, perspectives, and strategies that support increased capacity for all.

Duration

- May be a one-time peer learning event to address a specific issue, but generally forges ongoing partnerships for continued reflection, support, and problem solving that persist over time.

Delivery

- May occur face-to-face or through distance, technology-based, or hybrid methods.

Education Definitions

Intersections between training, technical assistance and post-secondary education

Though one method of PD delivery is generally predominant in a given situation, *training, technical assistance and education frequently overlap.* All three of these may be organized and sponsored by institutions of higher education. College and university instructors may be engaged in delivery of all three types of PD. Many college students are already working in the field and may be participating in training or TA as part of or parallel to degree completion.

For example, all teacher education programs include *practical training*, sometimes called clinical practice, field experience, internship, co-op, or student teaching. All teacher education programs include observation, supervision, feedback, and reflection on practice as part of this clinical practice. Higher education institutions often include a *campus lab school or children's center* in which the children's teachers, college students and college instructors observe, practice and reflect together on their work with young children.

In addition, many colleges and universities have *partnerships* with school districts, Head Start or other community agencies to organize student teaching practice, reflection, coaching and mentoring from faculty and experienced peers. Early childhood faculty may be important partners in the transition of recent education program graduates into their first teaching positions, through *new teacher induction programs.* They may participate as mentors or coaches in state or community quality improvement and professional development initiatives.

Many *teachers already working in the field take college coursework as part of their ongoing professional development.* They may take individual courses to refresh, expand or update knowledge and practice, earning college credit. Or, they may complete an educational certificate or degree program to renew certification, earn a new credential or to prepare for a new professional role in the field. Higher education institutions often include a division of *Continuing Education or Adult Education* that offers credit and noncredit courses for students who do not seek to complete a degree program but want the sustained training offered through individual courses or *certificate programs.*

Relevant Federal Legislation and Research Centers

Higher education is part of the federal and state elementary, secondary and postsecondary education system. Though workforce and higher education language varies from state to state, most of the definitions used here are established in federal and state education systems and legislation including

Higher Education Act of 1965, most recently amended in 2008. http://www2.ed.gov/policy/highered/leg/hea08/index.html

Carl D. Perkins Career and Technical Education Improvement Act http://www2.ed.gov/policy/sectech/leg/perkins/index.html

Workforce Investment Partnership Act http://thomas.loc.gov/cgi-bin/bdquery/z?d105:HR01385:ITOM:/bss/d105query.htmll

Integrated Postsecondary Education Data System (IPEDS). Sponsored by the U.S. Department of Education (DoE) / Institute of Education Sciences (IES) / National Center for Educational Statistics (NCES) http://nces.ed.gov/ipeds/glossary/

Definitions

Education is a series of learning experiences with related assessments of learning; specific to an area of inquiry and related set of skills or dispositions; delivered by a professional(s) with subject matter and adult learning knowledge and skills; and offered by an accredited school, college or university. A planned sequence of courses, along with admission and graduation requirements, comprises an *education program.*

Postsecondary education or higher education follows elementary and secondary education and is defined by IPEDS as "formal instructional programs with a curriculum designed primarily for students who are beyond compulsory age for high school."

Correspondence education is defined in the Higher Education Act as self paced education in which the institution of higher education (IHE) provides instructional materials and assessments, using postal mail or electronic methods. Interaction between the student and instructor or other students is minimal and not substantive. (Higher Education Act of 2008, section 602.3)

Distance education is defined in the Higher Education Act as relationship-based education in which the IHE provides synchronous or asynchronous methods that fit into course credit, semester, trimester or quarter structures. There is substantive and frequent interaction between students and between the student and the instructor. Distance education may use any of these technologies: the internet, satellite, cable, video cast, podcast, CD and DVD. Distance education programs may be conducted through exclusively distance methods or through blended or hybrid methods that combine distance and face-to-face coursework. . (Higher Education Act of 2008, section 602.3)

Institutions of Higher Education (IHEs) are defined in the Higher Education Act, Title 34, Part 600 as education institutions (schools, colleges and universities) that provide postsecondary education, beyond elementary and secondary education. IHEs include community colleges; public and private colleges; public and private universities; and some technical, career and business schools. IHEs may be federally designated as Tribal Colleges and Universities, Historically Black Community Colleges and Universities (HBCCUs), and Hispanic Serving Institutions (HSIs).

To be eligible for federal funds including student grants and loans, IHEs must be legally autho-rized by a state agency, admit only students who have a high school diploma or equivalent, provide educational programs that award associate, baccalaureate or graduate degrees, and be accredited by an agency approved by the U.S. Department of Education or are approved by a state agency. (Title 34, Part 600) IHEs also offer workforce, vocational and continuing education programs of one year or less (often called diploma or certificate programs); and offer both credit and non-credit courses.

Instructors, Professors, Field Supervisors, and other Faculty members are employees of IHEs assigned to a department or program(s). They are hired according to state, institution and accreditation requirements and meet the qualifications of those requirements. Institutional accreditors generally require that faculty have graduate degrees in the subjects that they teach, or in a closely related field. Some accreditors define closely related fields as those with at least 18 graduate credits in the field.

College credits, courses and semesters are defined in federal, state and institution regulations and guidelines. A typical course is 3 credit hours or 3 hours of instructor-student contact per week over a 15-week period. Students are expected to engage in substantive, additional, independent learning assignments for each course, each week. A typical semester is 15 weeks of class sessions, plus a 16th week of final exams. A full time course load for undergraduates is 12-15 credits per semester. Courses at institutions on a trimester or quarter schedule may have different configurations. For example, a typical quarter system is 11 weeks long, with a full time course load of 14-18 credits per quarter.

Direct assessment methods are defined in the Higher Education Act as methods that award course credit to students who demonstrate evidence that they have already mastered course content and requirements. Direct assessment may be 1) a direct assessment of the individual student's knowledge, skills or 2) direct assessment of another training or education program or course, along with evidence that the student met performance expectations. (Higher Education Act of 2008, section 602.3) Direct assessment of student mastery may include credit for prior learning as measured by exams, portfolios, and teaching performance evaluations.

Degree Program/Program of Study/Higher Education Programs

Degree Program/Program of Study/Higher Education Programs are defined in the Higher Education Act as "postsecondary education programs offered by an institution of higher education that leads to an academic of professional degree, certificate or other recognized educational credential." (Higher Education Act of 2008, section 602.3)

Program Graduates or Program Completers are those students who complete all components of a specific program of study; meet expectations on key assessments often related to institution, state or national standards; meet academic expectations related to grade point averages and timely progress toward program completion; and other graduation requirements. Students who are actively enrolled in a program but have not yet completed program requirements are generally referred to as *candidates*.

Teacher Education Programs are programs of study organized in a coherent and sequential program of coursework that includes individual study, peer learning, field experiences and performance assessments. These learning experiences are facilitated and assessed by course instructors who are employed by an institution of higher education (IHE).

Many IHEs offer shorter certificate programs, programs that satisfy requirements for CDA training, ongoing professional development for current teachers, or programs that provide alternate pathways to professional roles for career changers. Successful program completers earn specialized degrees, diplomas, or certificates that may lead to national or state early childhood credentials or meet other requirements for professional roles.

Alternate route programs are post-baccalaureate programs designed for individuals who have undergraduate degrees in areas other than teacher education. Alternate route programs may include teacher residency programs, worksite based programs, Teach for America, and Troops to Teachers. When these programs include *nontraditional providers*, this should be in partnership with accredited IHEs

and with accountability measures comparable to traditional postsecondary education programs.

Tech-Prep programs are defined in the Carl D. Perkins Act as programs of study that combine at least two years of secondary (high school) education with a minimum of two yeas of postsecondary education. These programs combine academic and vocational instruction, may be worksite based, and lead to a college degree or vocational certificate. They lead to immediate placement in a specialized career and/or to further postsecondary education. (Carl D. Perkins Act Section 203)

Field experiences and clinical practice includes field observations, field work, practica, student teaching and other "clinical" practice experiences such as home visiting. A planned sequence of these experiences supports student development of understanding, competence and dispositions in a specialized area of practice. (NAEYC 2010 Initial and Advanced Standards)

Lab Schools and Campus Children's Centers offer educational programs to children on college campuses. They may serve children of the students and staff who study or work at the institution, as well as local community children. They may include childcare services, preschool and prekindergarten services, and elementary grades. In some cases, they include licensed infant and toddler programs, Head Start programs or state approved elementary schools. These programs often serve as observation and field sites for teacher education students. Early childhood faculty may work as teachers, supervisors, technical assistance providers or coaches in campus lab schools and children's centers.

State approval is generally required for a community college, university or other IHE to offer early childhood degree programs as part of a state higher education system. State approval of specific degree programs may be required for graduates to be eligible for state teacher licensure. State approved *alternate routes* to licensure usually exist for those "career changers" who already have a degree in another field. State approval may be offered by the state Department of Education, Department of Higher Education, Board of Regents, or other state higher education system agency. State approval of professional preparation programs typically requires or encourages *national program accreditation*.

National Accreditation or Recognition is public recognition of IHEs and professional degree programs awarded by non-governmental agencies through a process of standard setting, self study, peer review, accreditation decision, and ongoing reporting.

> ***National Accreditation of institutions*** is a well-established means of monitoring the quality of IHEs and the educational programs that they offer. The Higher Education Act of 1965 and its reauthorizations require that federal student grants and loans may go only to those IHEs that are accredited by agencies recognized by the U.S. Department of Education. Four year institutions accredited by The National Council for Accreditation of Teacher Education (NCATE) are recognized by the U.S. Department of Education.

> ***National Accreditation of Professional Programs*** is valued in many states, by many employers, and by students. In most established professions, licensed practitioners are required to meet national professional standards and completion of a degree program accredited by the national profession is required before taking licensure exams. The National Council for Accreditation of Teacher Education (NCATE) recognizes NAEYC as the national professional standard setting agency for early childhood teacher education programs.
>
> > • Early childhood *associate degree programs* in IHE's earn accreditation from the NAEYC Commission on Early Childhood Associate Degree Accreditation (ECADA).

> • NAEYC also offers recognition to those *baccalaureate and graduate degree programs* that meet NAEYC standards and are sponsored by a department or school of education that is accredited by the National Council for Accreditation of Teacher Education (NCATE). However, NCATE accreditation of an IHE alone does not earn NAEYC recognition or indicate that NAEYC professional preparation standards are met.

Credentials are academic degrees, licenses or certificates awarded to individuals who successfully complete state or national requirements to enter specialized roles in the early childhood profession.

> ***State Teacher Licensure*** is the process used by a state governmental agency to grant professional recognition to individuals who meet state requirements to teach in a specialized teaching discipline, such as early childhood or special education. State credentials may be called certificates or licenses.

> ***Professional Certification*** is the process used by a non-governmental state or national agency to grant professional recognition to individuals who meet the requirements of the agency. The Council for Professional Recognition and the National Board for Professional Teaching Standards offer national early childhood credentials.

Induction programs are comprehensive staff development programs designed by a school or other employer to support, train and retain first year teachers. Induction programs may be part of professional or leadership development plans and can include peer-to-peer networks, teacher learning communities, mentoring, and coaching. Induction programs are often a partnership between the IHE and school or other early education setting, supporting the college students' transition from clinical practice as part of degree completion to first years of work in a new professional role.

Additional Characteristics of Postsecondary Education Programs

Focus

- *Initial teacher education programs* prepare candidates for first early childhood teaching licensure (pre-service education) or for settings that do not require licensure. They may be offered at associate, baccalaureate or graduate degree levels.

- *Advanced teacher education programs* prepare candidates for advanced positions in the field such as accomplished or mentor early childhood teacher, early childhood administrator, state early childhood specialists, teacher educators and researchers. They are offered at master's and doctoral levels.

- *In-service or Continuing Education* is PD in which early childhood professionals enhance their skills and maintain current knowledge and practice. Continuing education may be required in order to maintain individual licensure or advance to a new level of licensure, to meet employer expectations, or to meet other local, state or federal requirements for early childhood professionals working in the field.

- *All teacher education programs* provide learning experiences and performance-based assessments of individual learning related to understanding young children, their families and communities; child assessment; planning and implementing effective practices; mastering and applying academic content disciplines; and professional responsibilities. These components are shared by the national CDA competencies, InTASC standards, NCATE standards, and NAEYC professional preparation standards.

Relationships

- All education programs are strengthened by trusting and respectful interactions *between instructor and student, and between students*. Because educational programs include multiple sessions, students benefit from intentionally developed opportunities to build positive relationships between and among instructors(s) and participants.

- All teacher education programs benefit from reciprocal, respectful relationships between *the IHE, the early childhood degree program, and community field sites*. Individuals and organization partners value each other as resources for learning, for sharing expertise, and for strengthening each other's work.

- All education programs benefit from engagement with *community stakeholders*. In early childhood programs, representatives from the following stakeholder groups are typically invited to participate in a formal advisory group: program alumni, employers of program graduates, community child care and Head Start programs, local school districts, local businesses, NAEYC affiliates or chapters, and local or state early childhood initiatives.

- Relationships *between students* are facilitated through peer tutoring programs and study groups; student clubs; online discussions and social networking; mentoring from students who have successfully completed a course, completed the program, or transferred to a higher level degree or institution; and cohorts of students that share common challenges and support each other through the duration of the program.

- Early childhood programs also foster relationships *between students and the larger early childhood professional community* through facilitation of Early Childhood Student Club activities, field placements, job fairs, graduation ceremonies, and capstone portfolio reviews.

Process

- *Program design, course design, and instructor teaching strategies* incorporate adult learning principles including interactive learning activities, exercises, and instructional aids (handouts, audiovisuals, and other components of instruction) to facilitate learning experiences that support defined outcomes.

- *Faculty engage in* reflective practice both individually and with peer instructors, including reflection on own practices, observation of peers, observation and feedback from peers, and other evaluations. Program faculty use student performance data to inform decisions about program design, course design, teaching and learning.

- *Students engage in* substantive, meaningful independent or group learning projects each week, in addition to instructor contact time.

- *Student advising* helps students understand program requirements and institution process and procedures. Faculty and admissions office staff work together to plan and offer student advising that is responsive to the needs of the early childhood program and its students. Stable faculty members advise the students over time to support faculty-student mentoring relationships.

- *Completion* of education coursework leads to college credit. Completion of education programs leads to a credential, certificate, diploma or degree. These should be embedded in the recipient's broader professional development plan.

Duration

- *Credit, course, semester, and program duration* meets institution, state and federal requirements. An associate degree is at least 60 credit hours of college level course work. A bachelor's degree is at least 120 credit hours of college level course work. A master's degree can be an additional 30-50 credits depending on focus and certifications.

- To support *student retention and timely completion*, IHEs offer a range of services including admission and financial aid offices, student learning centers, easily accessible catalogs of program requirements and semester offerings, advising related to program progress and course selection, and advising related to long term career planning.

- To preserve the meaning and *integrity of the diploma or other credential* 1) All program completers meet comparable and objective performance standards. 2) Duration depends upon academic readiness and progress. 3) Developmental or remedial courses do not count as college credit. 4) College credit is earned only for satisfactory grades. 5) There are limits on the number of times a student can retake a course. 6) Each course counts only one time.

- *Traditional teacher education programs* offered on the IHE campus, work in close collaboration with multiple community field sites to plan and implement student field observation and practice assignments. There are multiple opportunities for face-to-face interaction between faculty and students, and between students. Early childhood students are encouraged to engage in campus life beyond class attendance.

- *Correspondence education* is self-paced with minimal interaction between the student and instructor or peers. It should not be considered the first choice for most students and should not comprise an entire early childhood teacher education program. Where correspondence courses are offered, students are encouraged to engage in peer and instructor interaction beyond the course structure.

- *Distance education* offers asynchronous schedules and minimal travel to campus. The design is relationship-based with substantive and frequent interaction between students and between the student and the instructor. Distance technologies (the internet, satellite, cable, video cast, podcast, CD and DVD) are chosen for best fit to course content and processes and for accessibility to all demographic student groups.

- *Key assessments* should be aligned with national standards and implemented consistently across all course sections and delivery methods. *Direct assessment* methods may be used to award credit in lieu of course completion when students can demonstrate mastery of course content and requirements. This may be through 1) "testing out" of a course through satisfactory performance on one or more key assessments or 2) "transfer in" of a course from another training or education program. When there is not a one-to-one course match, direct assessments should consider equivalency of blocks of courses or of programs as a whole, focusing on course assessments or outcomes rather than course numbers, titles or other inputs.

- *Field or clinical experiences* help students develop professional skills and dispositions, understanding and integrating theory and practice. These experiences begin early in the program and lead to capstone experiences, helping students to integrate the content and practice components of each course and to build increasing competence over time. Across all delivery methods, there are clear expectations for field sites, with substantive and frequent interaction between instructor and cooperating teachers and administrators in the field. Cohorts of students interact regularly to share experiences, reflect on practice, and receive guidance and mentoring from both master teachers and faculty. Faculty supervisors regularly observe student practice and communicate with cooperating teachers and administrators. Over time, partnerships with field sites support professional relationships and ongoing improvements in both programs – the adult education program and the children's early learning program. Field and clinical experiences are implemented with comparable methods and resources across different sites and across local and distance programs.

APPENDICES

Appendix A—Technical Assistance Strategies with Implications for Postsecondary Education Programs
Mentoring, Coaching and Consultation are strategies common to early childhood training and education programs. This table is designed to allow easy comparison between and among these strategies, which are often similar in practice and intent and often overlap in practice. Because these strategies are often integrated into the clinical practice components of postsecondary education programs, the last row in the table identifies some implications for implementation of these strategies in higher education.

Technical Assistance Strategies with Implications for Postsecondary Education Programs

	Mentoring	Coaching	Consultation
Definition	Mentoring is a relationship-based process between colleagues in similar professional roles, with a more-experienced individual with adult learning knowledge and skills, the mentor, providing guidance and example to the less-experienced protégé or mentee. Mentoring is intended to increase an individual's personal or professional capacity, resulting in greater professional effectiveness.	Coaching is a relationship-based process led by an expert with specialized and adult learning knowledge and skills, who often serves in a different professional role than the recipient(s). Coaching is designed to build capacity for specific professional dispositions, skills, and behaviors and is focused on goal-setting and achievement for an individual or group.	Consultation is a collaborative, problem-solving process between an external consultant with specific expertise and adult learning knowledge and skills and an individual or group from one program or organization. Consultation facilitates the assessment and resolution of an issue-specific concern—a program-/organizational-, staff-, or child-/family-related issue—or addresses a specific topic.
Focus	Addresses a specific topic or the protégé's holistic professional growth. Supports the reflective processes that professionals need to translate the theories and information learned through education and/or training into best practices. Should be included in the recipient's broader professional development plan.	Supports the development of specific skills and practices; it is focused on a performance-based outcome(s). Should be embedded in the recipient's broader professional development plan that provides the theoretical foundations related to the specific skills being addressed.	Resolution of a specific concern or set of concerns. Capacity-building approach to facilitate the recipient's continued use of the process employed during or as a result of the consultation.
Relationships	Includes the mentor and protégé establishing and maintaining a positive, trusting, and respectful relationship. Ideal match up of mentor and protégé is mutually agreed upon rather than assigned. A person may also enlist a mentor, be assigned to a mentor, or the mentor may be assigned to an individual. Can be accomplished by some supervisors, but should be distinguished from supervisory processes. Should not be used as a method of evaluating job performance.	Requires interactions that build trust and respect. A person may select a coach, be assigned to a coach, or the coach may be assigned to an individual or group. Should be distinguished from supervisory processes; however, its findings and conclusions may contribute to job performance evaluation. In these instances, the recipient of the coaching should be made aware of this possibility.	Requires a collaborative relationship between the consultant and the person to whom he/she provides recommendations. Consultants may be engaged by the administrative leadership of a workplace. In some instances the consultancy is arranged or directed by a regulatory or funding agency or organization.

Process	Begins with establishing role clarity and goal setting.	Begins with a collaborative agreement between the coach and the individual to set the guidelines and goals.	Begins with the joint development of goals.
	Includes the facilitation of adult learning techniques such as guided self-reflection, resulting in the application of new ideas to the protégé's professional practice or personal disposition.	Includes various combinations of questioning, listening, observation, reflection, feedback, prompting, modeling, and practice.	Supports the development of goal-related solutions and the implementation strategies recommended to achieve them. Recommendations may include the provisions of other relationship-based TA methods.
	May include unplanned contacts between mentor and protégé when the protégé has questions or specific concerns.	Likely to occur through planned onsite contacts.	Likely to occur through planned onsite contacts.
	Remains ongoing or concludes by mutual consent or when the protégé has achieved her goals	Concludes when the specified goal has been achieved.	Concludes with a summary process and an evaluation of the effectiveness of the consultation provided.
Duration	Ongoing, iterative process.	Can occur one time or in a series of sessions, dependent upon the successful achievement of the goal.	Generally short term. Long-term relationships with consultants may develop if individuals, programs, or organizations use them for assistance in addressing multiple, often interrelated, concerns over time. As an example, long-term relationships with consultants may evolve as they help guide overall program quality improvement processes.
Delivery	May be provided face-to-face (onsite or offsite) or through distance, technology-based, or hybrid methods.	May be provided face-to-face (onsite or offsite) or through distance, technology-based, or hybrid methods.	May be provided face-to-face (onsite or offsite) or through distance, technology-based, or hybrid methods.

Implications for Education Programs

Students frequently turn to instructors as mentors, seeking advice related to current professional or family situations, career opportunities and direction, and issues related to the ways that higher education experience can change personal identity and relationships. These mentor relationships can last for many years after the student completes the program.

Because childcare and Head Start settings do not have the same entry requirements as P-12 schools, students working in childcare and Head Start may already hold teacher or administrator roles when they begin their college education.

Additionally, as the average age of college students rises, faculty and students are often age peers. This is especially true in community colleges.

In this sense, students may have both a mentor and peer relationship with the college instructor.

Faculty members regularly engage in coaching as they observe students in field or clinical settings and facilitate skill building and reflection on practice.

Adjunct faculty may hold jobs in the field and are occasionally the employer of one or more of their students. All instructors have the responsibility to fairly evaluate student work in ways that will affect the student's progress through the program. Students are aware of this aspect of the coaching relationship.

Meeting course and degree program requirements is an explicit component of the coaching relationship guidelines and goals. An ongoing challenge is to make course expectations clear and evaluate students objectively, while simultaneously supporting honest, reflective practice.

Faculty members do not directly engage in consulting contracts with students. However, many instructors do serve as consultants to early learning programs in their community. In this case, the instructor's consulting relationship is probably with a program administrator.

Often the same program administrators that seek support from consultants are the programs that encourage continuing education for staff and are engaged in a partnership with the education program as a field site or advisory group member.

It is not uncommon for a faculty member to be serving as a consultant to an early learning program that employs his or her past, current and future students or that serves as a field site for the adult education program. It is especially important to be aware of potential conflicts of interest if an instructor engages in a direct consulting arrangement with a current student

Appendix B—Project Overview and Process

One of NAEYC's three broad goals is to improve professional practice and working conditions in early childhood education. In support of this goal, NAEYC's governing board and staff review and discuss ways to enhance quality early childhood professional development. In 2009 creating a cross-sector framework for role, function, and core capabilities for those who provide professional development was identified as an important issue that could be immediately addressed.

Early Childhood Education Professional Development: Training and Technical Assistance Definitions

From 2009 through mid-2010 NAEYC hosted multiple focus groups and facilitated input sessions on states' critical policy questions, strategies, challenges, ideas, and needs related to professional development methods and the core capabilities of those who provide it. Several of these sessions were convened with national partners including NACCRRA, the National Professional Development Center on Inclusion, and National Louis University: McCormick Center for Early Childhood Leadership. Participants in these focus groups included representatives from all sectors of the early childhood field (e.g., child care, Head Start, schools, early intervention) and its varied roles, including direct service practitioners (center- and school-based teachers and family child care providers); those who provide professional development and supports (trainers, technical assistance providers, mentors, coaches, consultants, advisors, higher education faculty, and others); program, agency, and system administrators; national, state and local policy makers; and researchers both within and from outside of the early education field.

During this year-and-a-half dialogue, three main issues were consistently raised as most urgent:

- consistent, national definitions and standards to help further clarify and move forward state and local efforts, particularly in relation to technical assistance (including mentoring, coaching, consultation, and advising);

- core competencies for those who provide professional development; and

- evaluating, measuring, and tracking training and technical assistance.

In February 2010 NACCRRA partnered with NAEYC in a joint effort to develop national definitions for training and technical assistance. The two organizations spent several months engaged in a review of new and historically significant related research as well as existing state definitions and associated quality improvement and assurance efforts. The organizations decided that this joint work should start from where states' system policy efforts are, using practice and system policies as a foundation for definitions development; the project lens and focus was practice and state policy-based. During the drafting process the definitions work expanded to include training, TA, *and* education definitions, as well as contextual information about the early education field and workforce.

In September 2010 an early draft was circulated for review and feedback to key experts representing early childhood researchers, national and state technical assistance networks, state professional development system administrators, policy consultants, and higher education faculty. A second early draft was also used for a state feedback discussion at The National Registry Alliance annual conference in late September. From October through December 2010 targeted feedback was solicited from additional key national organization and association partners, including ACCESS and the National Association for Early Childhood Teacher Educators (NAECTE), and state stakeholders representing the varied roles of the field.

Early Childhood Education Professional Development: Education Definitions

Based on the feedback provided, as well as the time-sensitive needs expressed by state policy and system administrators, NAEYC and NACCRRA decided to move forward with the finalization of the glossary of training and TA definitions. NAEYC and the Alliance of Early Childhood Teacher Educators continued to explore and develop national education-related definitions for the next edition of the glossary. Early drafts were developed by a workgroup that included NAEYC staff, ACCESS and NAECTE board members representing the Alliance of Early Childhood Teacher Educators. Development of definitions included a review of recent teacher education research and policy papers as well as terminology established in current federal legislation. Final input was solicited from ACCESS and NAECTE members and during a national feedback discussion at the 2011 NAEYC Annual Conference.

During this twelve-month dialogue, work focused on

1. Additional contextual definitions that provide common understandings of terminology used in P-12 and postsecondary education policy and practice

2. Shared understanding of and vision for characteristics of postsecondary education programs

3. Recognition that technical assistance strategies are often embedded into clinical practice components of teacher education programs and related implications

A writing group took on the task of gathering input and completing the education definitions. The Writing Group members were Nancy Beaver, Eastfield College, Dallas Community College District; Sara Davis, University of Arkansas-Fort Smith; Libby Etheridge, University of Oklahoma; Nancy Freeman, University of South Carolina; Carrie Nepstad, Harold Washington College, City Colleges of Chicago; and Alison Lutton, NAEYC staff.

Acknowledgments

NAEYC, the Alliance, and NACCRRA thank the hundreds of state experts and national colleagues that shared their ideas, needs, and hopes related to this work. We sincerely hope this glossary helps us all in our efforts to improve the quality of practice and supports available to our nation's early education workforce.

Specifically, we thank state policy maker and PD leadership representatives from 44 states and the District of Columbia, and the following national organizations/agencies, for their participation in input and feedback processes.

- ACCESS–Associate Degree Early Childhood Teacher Educators
- Center for the Study of Child Care Employment
- Child Trends
- Division for Early Childhood of the Council for Exceptional Children
- NACCRRA–National Association of Child Care Resource and Referral Agencies
- National Association for Family Child Care
- National Association of Early Childhood Teacher Educators
- National Association of Early Childhood Specialists in State Departments of Education
- National Center for Children in Poverty
- National Child Care Information and Technical Assistance Center
- National Louis University: McCormick Center for Early Childhood Leadership
- National Professional Development Center on Inclusion
- The National Registry Alliance
- Office of Head Start
- Society for Research in Child Development
- U.S. Department of Education
- Zero to Three

Additional gratitude is extended to NAEYC Affiliate's volunteer and staff leadership, NACCRRA state networks and Child Care Resource and Referral agencies' leadership and staff, and the leadership of the Alliance of Early Childhood Teacher Educators (a collaborative effort of the National Association of Early Childhood Teacher Educators [NAECTE] and Associate Degree Early Childhood Teacher Educators [ACCESS]).

NAEYC also thanks the Birth to Five Policy Alliance and the McCormick Foundation whose generosity helped to support NAEYC's role in this project.

Training and Technical Assistance Glossary jointly authored by the National Association for the Education of Young Children and the National Association of Child Care Resource and Referral Agencies

Adult Education Glossary jointly authored by the National Association for the Education of Young Children and the Alliance of Early Childhood Teacher Educators (a collaborative effort of the National Association of Early Childhood Teacher Educators [NAECTE] and Associate Degree Early Childhood Teacher Educators [ACCESS])

Alison Lutton

Using the New NAEYC
Professional Preparation Standards

What does it mean to be a qualified, well-prepared early childhood professional?

What does excellent teaching in early childhood look like? What role should standards play in our profession? In his editorial opening to a special issue of the international journal *Contemporary Issues in Early Childhood*, Mathias Urban writes,

> Care and education for young children, and the social institutions we construct around early childhood, lie at the very heart of any human society—they define what we are (here and now), and what we aspire to become as a society. . . . These ways of understanding, too, shape our concepts of what it means to be, to become, and to act professionally in working with young children, families, and communities (2010, 2).

One of the ways we describe professionalism is to identify essential elements of what early childhood professionals should know and be able to do, across our many different professional roles and settings and across the early childhood period of human development from birth through age 8. The NAEYC position statement "NAEYC Standards for Early Childhood Professional Preparation Programs" (NAEYC 2009) expresses these essentials. The standards provide a national vision for all early childhood professionals, whether they work in child care centers or homes, Head Start, or preK–4 classrooms. The standards define an essential common core of knowledge and practice for all training and education programs that prepare early childhood teachers, researchers, policy makers, and teacher educators. They present a shared vision of excellence for all who work with young children.

The early childhood field puts the NAEYC standards to use in NAEYC accreditation and recognition of training and education programs, in development and ongoing improvement of early childhood degree programs, in state approvals of teacher education programs, and in state professional development systems. These standards apply across all early childhood training and education programs, across all degree and licensure levels, and for those considering entry into the field as well as for those who seek to enhance their practice or prepare for new roles.

Thirty years of NAEYC standards

The NAEYC Governing Board approved the first standards in 1981 and published them the next year, *Early Childhood Teacher Education Guidelines for Four- and Five-Year Programs*. Three more position statements on standards quickly followed: "Guidelines for Early Childhood Education Programs in Associate Degree Granting Institutions" (1984), "Developmentally Appropriate Practice in Early Childhood Programs Serving Children from Birth through Age 8" (1986), and "Developmentally Appropriate Practice in the Primary Grades Serving 5- through 8-Year-Olds" (1988) (NAEYC 2001, 21–25). The position statement "Guidelines for Appropriate Curriculum Content and Assessment in Programs Serving Children Ages 3 through 8" was adopted (1990) and published in 1992 in *Reaching Potentials: Appropriate Curriculum and Assessment for Young Children, Volume 1.*

During the 1980s, NAEYC launched the Council for Professional Recognition, created the NAEYC Academy as an accreditation system for programs serving young children, and became a constituent member of the National Council for the Accreditation of Teacher Education (NCATE). Through the NCATE partnership, NAEYC began to offer national recognition to baccalaureate and graduate degree programs that meet NAEYC standards (NAEYC 2001).

The 1982 teacher education guidelines were revised in 1996 and 2001, and again in 2009. Each revision process included input from advisory groups, participants in conference sessions, related early childhood organizations, specialty area associations such as the Division for Early Childhood (DEC) of the Council for Exceptional Children, and other teacher-accrediting or -credentialing organizations such as the National Board for Professional Teaching Standards (NBPTS). Each revision responded to changes in the field, often making conceptual shifts. The 1996 revision reflected the shift toward providing services for young children with disabilities and developmental delays in inclusive early childhood programs. Those revisions clarified that

> Early childhood settings [include] but [are] not limited to any part- or full-time program in a center, school, or home that serves children from birth through age 8 and their families, including children with special developmental and learning needs.

This definition includes programs in child care centers, for both profit and nonprofit; private and public prekindergarten programs; Head Start programs; family child care; and kindergartens, primary grades, and before- and after-school programs in elementary schools. (NAEYC 1996, 3)

The 1996 revisions framed the guidelines as outcomes rather than processes, reflecting shifts under way across the preK–20 education systems.

The 2001 revisions continued the movement toward more performance-based standards. The evidence submitted by programs seeking NAEYC recognition shifted from portfolios to evidence of the program's implementation of the assessments aligned with NAEYC performance standards, along with aggregate data on student performance by standard. Programs received time to transition to this new approach, but soon were able to submit a set of aligned assessments, student performance data, and reflections on the use of that data as part of ongoing program improvement. The revisions also reflected NAEYC's work with leaders in the field to develop a system for Early Childhood Associate Degree Accreditation (ECADA). The associate degree standards included a strengthened section on the role of community colleges and the need to provide substantive early childhood course work and field experience to improve the practice of those already in the field, while keeping open the doors to possible program transfers from associate to baccalaureate.

The percentage of White early childhood teachers increases as degree requirements and compensation rise (Chang 2006). The early childhood field needs to simultaneously increase diversity, education levels, and compensation in the early childhood workforce. Community colleges that support alignment of associate degree programs with national standards have a decisive role to play (Lutton 2009). Community colleges remain critical to building a more diverse teaching workforce, enrolling 52 percent of all Native American, 45 percent of all Asian/Pacific Islander, 45 percent of all Black, and 53 percent of all Hispanic undergraduate students in the United States (AACC 2009).

What's new in the standards?

The most recent revisions to the professional preparation standards appear in the 2009 position statement "NAEYC Standards for Early Childhood Professional Preparation Programs." These revisions consider the ways that the early childhood professional landscape has changed over the past decade. Final revisions in 2009 focus on four changes in the landscape.

Increasing diversity in young children. Nearly one in four children in the United States lives in a first- or second-generation immigrant family. Over a third of those children have at least one parent born in Mexico. Twenty-two percent of all children in the United States are Hispanic. Fifty-six percent are non-Hispanic White. Fifteen percent of all children are non-Hispanic Black and four percent are non-Hispanic Asian/Pacific Islander. The percentages of children who are Hispanic, who are Asian/Pacific Islander, and who identify as more than one race are expected to continue to grow (Child Trends Data Bank 2009). There are strong indications that early childhood teacher education programs need to make improvements in order to prepare teacher candidates for this diversity in children and families (Ray et al. 2006).

RESPONSE TO THIS ISSUE. After much discussion about the possibility of a new standard focused on diversity, the NAEYC Standards Position Statement Work Group affirmed the approach of integrating diversity into every standard as having more potential strength. The group acknowledged that preparation to support diverse children, families, and communities in inclusive settings needed to be strengthened in the education of early childhood professionals. This requires more intentional training of NAEYC reviewers and more intentional presentation of evidence by professional training and educa-

Early Childhood Leaders Work Three Years to Develop the Standards for Professional Preparation Programs

While hundreds of individuals helped to develop the NAEYC standards by providing valuable input during meetings at national conferences and by submitting input during public comment periods, the following groups participated in multiple meetings to develop the position statement and related degree-level expectations over a three-year period.

NAEYC Standards Position Statement Work Group, 2008–2009

Rebecca Brinks, Grand Rapids Community College, Michigan
Julie Bullard, University of Montana–Western
Josué Cruz, Council for Professional Recognition, Washington, D.C.
Sharon Fredericks, College of Menominee Nation, Wisconsin
John Johnston, University of Memphis, Tennessee
Frances O'Connell Rust, Erikson Institute, Illinois
Ursula Thomas-Fair, University of West Georgia

NAEYC Commission on Early Childhood Associate Degree Accreditation, 2008–2010

Tracey Bennet, Vance-Granville Community College, North Carolina
Rebecca Brinks, Grand Rapids Community College, Michigan
Isela Castañon-Williams, El Paso Community College, Texas
Camille Catlett, Frank Porter Graham Child Development Institute, North Carolina
Rebecca Gorton, Northampton Community College, Pennsylvania
Elisa Huss-Hage, Owens Community College, Ohio
John Johnston, University of Memphis, Tennessee
Deborah Jordan, Council for Professional Recognition, Washington, D.C.
Christina Lopez Morgan, DeAnza Community College, California
Toni Ungaretti, Johns Hopkins University, Maryland

NAEYC Initial and Advanced Program Audit Team, 2008–2010

Julie Bullard, University of Montana–Western
Ken Counselman, New Jersey City University
Sue George, Missouri State University
Rebecca Huss Keeler, University of Houston–Clear Lake, Texas
John Johnston, University of Memphis, Tennessee
Wendy McCarty, Illinois College
Julie Ray, Southeast Missouri State University
Terri Swim, Indiana University–Purdue University Fort Wayne

tion programs seeking NAEYC recognition or accreditation. Key elements and rubrics used by reviewers, auditors, and commissioners for each standard reflect this change.

Professional preparation in academic disciplines. The expectation that early childhood teachers should complete college degrees continues to grow. The 2007 Head Start reauthorization, research on professional preparation and teacher practices, national goals for a more highly educated workforce, federal and state policy emphasis on accountability and assessment, and the development of common core state standards for children's learning all raised the expectation that early childhood teachers should hold college degrees. At the same time, questions about the quality of early childhood teacher education programs emerged, including concerns about the preparation of early childhood teachers in academic disciplines such as language, literacy, math, science, and social studies (Willer et al. 2011).

RESPONSE TO THIS ISSUE. In response to concerns that early childhood teachers may not be adequately prepared in the academic disciplines, Standard 4 was separated into two standards, one focused on early childhood teaching methods (Standard 4) and a new standard focused on early childhood curriculum content (Standard 5). This ensures that both pedagogy and academic content receive focused attention and increases the total number of core standards to six. Key elements and rubrics used by reviewers, auditors, and commissioners for each standard reflect this change.

State alignment of professional training and education programs with NAEYC standards. The 1984 "Guidelines for Early Childhood Education Programs in Associate Degree Granting Institutions" recognized that many promising current and future members of our field begin their initial, formal early childhood studies with an associate degree from their local community college. The introduction to the 2003 position statement "NAEYC Standards for Early Childhood Professional Preparation: Associate Degree Programs" emphasized that while some students needed academic or English language support at college entry, successful graduates of strong associate degree

level programs were ready to continue their education in bachelor degree programs (NAEYC 2003). By 2010, the NAEYC Commission on Early Childhood Associate Degree Accreditation accredited 114 associate degree level programs in 24 states, with an additional 145 programs engaged in self-study. In 34 states, 363 baccalaureate and graduate programs received NAEYC recognition and NCATE accreditation. In many states, this rapid growth in NAEYC-accredited and -recognized professional preparation programs provides new opportunities to develop associate-to-baccalaureate transfer agreements based on alignment with NAEYC Initial Licensure program standards.

RESPONSE TO THIS ISSUE. The "2010 NAEYC Standards for Initial and Advanced Early Childhood Professional Preparation Programs," organized into a single document (NAEYC 2010) with one common introduction, creates a resource to be read and used by all professional development and preparation programs at all levels. It clearly supports the associate degree as one way to work toward completion of an initial early childhood preparation program. The 2010 program level standards explain how the NAEYC core standards in the 2009 position statement are met at initial and advanced degree levels. Key elements and rubrics used by reviewers, auditors, and commissioners for each program level are presented together, making it easier to see the progressively higher expectations in each standard. The Essential Professional Tools for All Candidates in Advanced Programs (NAEYC 2003, 77) are incorporated in the 2010 Advanced program key elements. The Initial program standards and rubric are used for all Initial programs, whether offered at associate, baccalaureate, or graduate levels.

Integration of professional standards across sectors. The need for more integrated professional development systems heightened as researchers and policy makers worked to connect the dots between quality rating and improvement systems (QRIS), professional development systems, and the variations in state standards and competencies (LeMoine 2008; LeMoine et al. 2011). As the field looked toward college degrees to raise program quality,

Overview of the National Board for Professional Teaching Standards'
Early Childhood Generalist Standards, Third Edition

In 2010, the National Board for Professional Teaching Standards (NBPTS) convened a committee of early childhood experts to review and revise the second edition of *Early Childhood Standards*. Teachers, higher education faculty, and other educators from local and state education agencies comprised the 14-member committee. Over the course of multiple meetings, the committee analyzed the current standards and revised them to reflect both the current state of the field and the anticipated trajectory of the field's growth over the next 10 years.

STANDARD I: Using Knowledge of Child Development to Understand the Whole Child. Accomplished early childhood teachers use their knowledge of child development to understand young children and to foster each child's development and learning.

STANDARD II: Partnering with Families and Communities. Accomplished early childhood teachers work reciprocally with families and community partners to support each child's development and learning and to advocate for young children and their families.

STANDARD III: Fostering Equity, Fairness, and Appreciation of Diversity. Accomplished early childhood teachers embrace diversity. They model and nurture treating others with equity, fairness, and dignity.

STANDARD IV: Knowing Subject Matter for Teaching Young Children. Accomplished early childhood teachers integrate the foundational ideas of the subjects they teach, the ways young children think about these ideas, and effective approaches to support each child's learning.

STANDARD V: Assessing Children's Development and Learning. Accomplished early childhood teachers use assessment to support and guide young children's development and learning.

STANDARD VI: Managing the Environment for Development and Learning. Accomplished early childhood teachers organize and manage the environment to promote young children's development and learning.

STANDARD VII: Planning for Development and Learning. Accomplished early childhood teachers plan for children's development and learning by setting developmentally appropriate goals and designing learning activities to achieve those goals.

STANDARD VIII: Implementing Instruction for Development and Learning. Accomplished early childhood teachers skillfully implement strategies and use resources to support young children's development and learning.

STANDARD IX: Reflecting on Teaching Young Children. Accomplished early childhood teachers engage in systematic reflection on their teaching to enhance their professional knowledge and skill and to benefit young children's development and learning.

STANDARD X: Exemplifying Professionalism and Contributing to the Profession. Accomplished early childhood teachers are leaders, collaborators, and advocates in improving early childhood programs, practices, and policies

Note: Early Childhood Generalist Standards, Third Edition, forthcoming in 2011, will serve as the basis for National Board Certification beginning in 2012. The standards and a list of standards and committee members are available on the NBPTS website. **www.nbpts.org/the_standards/standards_by_cert**.

it became increasingly clear that early child-hood teachers need early childhood specialization and should not have to get another degree to move between early childhood age groups or early learning settings. While optional concentrations in a specialized age group or role are valuable, early childhood degree programs need to prepare graduates for a lifelong career that can include movement across settings, roles, and age groups in the field.

RESPONSE TO THIS ISSUE. The 2009 position statement "NAEYC Standards for Early Childhood Professional Preparation Programs" reiterates the role of standards as a unifying vision that can support integration of the different systems and sectors that make up the early childhood field. The "2010 NAEYC Standards for Initial and Advanced Early Childhood Professional Preparation Programs" outlines requirements that all early childhood preparation programs include a birth through age 8 perspective in each standard, with field experiences in at least two of the three early learning settings (child care, Head Start, and preK–12 schools) and at least two of the three early childhood age groups (0–3, 3–5, 5–8). This expectation is presented as a new Standard 7 in the NAEYC Initial and Advanced standards adopted by the NCATE Specialty Area Standards Board. It is presented as Criterion 5 in the Associate Degree program standards adopted by the Commission on Early Childhood Associate Degree Accreditation.

Standards integration across systems

Standards are just one essential component of the systems needed to support developmentally effective teaching and learning. Essential components include the following:

• professional standards

• accredited training and education programs

• early childhood licensing and certification

• induction, mentoring, and coaching

• leadership in the early learning program

• adequate resources and working conditions

• ongoing professional development

• engagement in professional networks and associations

Three sets of national early childhood standards were recently revised or are currently under revision: (a) the NAEYC Professional Preparation standards, (b) the National Board for Professional Teaching Standards (NBPTS) Early Childhood Generalist standards, (c) and the Interstate Teacher Assessment and Support Consortium (InTASC) standards. The Council for Exceptional Children's national standards will be revised in the next few years. NAEYC's commitment to alignment with other national standards continues.

Cross-sector integration and alignment of national and state early childhood standards is one of the most pressing challenges facing our field. Differences persist in terminology, funding streams, regulations, approaches to measuring program quality, professional development structures, and licensing and credentialing systems. A set of unifying national standards, accompanied by accreditation for professional preparation programs that meet those standards, can help the early childhood field ensure well-prepared teachers for all children and their families. Program standards are more than a checklist. They are opportunities for stimulating creativity and innovation (Willer et al. 2011). A set of unifying professional early childhood standards is an important part of building a shared vision for our field that is both aspirational and achievable.

To learn more

InTASC (Interstate Assessment and Support Consortium). 2010. InTASC Model Core Teaching Standards: A Resource for State Dialogue. Draft document. Online: http://ccsso.org/resources/programs/interstate_teacher_assessment_consortium_(intasc).html.

NAEYC. 2009. NAEYC standards for early childhood professional preparation programs. Position Statement. Washington, DC: Author. Online: www.naeyc.org/positionstatements/ppp.

NBPTS (National Board for Professional Teaching Standards). 2010. Revisions to NBPTS early childhood generalist standards. Online: www.nbpts.org/the_standards/standards_by_cert.

Reprinted from *Young Children* 66 (2): 78–82.
Copyright © 2011 NAEYC.

References

AACC (American Association of Community Colleges). 2009. Fast facts—Demographics. Washington, DC: Author. www.aacc.nche.edu/AboutCC?pages/fastfacts.aspx.

Chang, H. 2006. *Getting ready for quality: The critical importance of developing and supporting a skilled, ethnically and linguistically diverse early childhood workforce.* Emeryville, CA: California Tomorrow.

Child Trends Data Bank. 2009. Racial and ethnic composition of the child population. www.childtrendsdatabank.org/?q=node/234.

LeMoine, S. 2008. *Workforce designs: A policy blueprint for state early childhood professional development systems.* Washington, DC: NAEYC.

LeMoine, S., A. Lutton, D. McDonald & J. Daniel. 2011. Integrating professional standards for the early childhood workforce: Putting the pieces together. In *Foundations for teaching excellence: Connecting early childhood quality rating, professional development, and competency systems in states*, eds. C. Howes & R.C. Pianta, 47–67. Baltimore, MD: Brookes.

Lutton, A. 2009. NAEYC early childhood professional preparation standards: A vision for tomorrow's early childhood teachers. In *Conversations on early childhood teacher education: Voices from the working forum for teacher educators*, eds. A. Gibbons & C. Gibbs, 29–36. Redmond, WA: World Forum Foundation; Auckland: New Zealand Tertiary College.

NAEYC. 1996. *Guidelines for preparation of early childhood professionals.* Washington, DC: Author.

NAEYC. 2001. *NAEYC at 75 years, 1926–2001: Reflections on the past, challenges for the future.* Washington, DC: Author.

NAEYC. 2003. *Preparing early childhood professionals: NAEYC standards for programs.* Washington, DC: Author.

NAEYC. 2009. NAEYC standards for early childhood professional preparation programs. Position statement. Washington, DC: Author. Online: www.naeyc.org/positionstatements/ppp.

NAEYC. 2010. 2010 NAEYC standards for initial and advanced early childhood professional preparation programs. Washington, DC: Author. Online: www.naeyc.org/ncate/standards.

Ray, A., B. Bowman, & J. Robbins. 2006. Preparing early childhood teachers to successfully educate all children: The contribution of state boards of higher education and national professional accreditation organizations, a project of the Initiative on Race, Class and Culture in Early Childhood. Final report. New York: Foundation for Child Development.

Urban, M., 2010. Editorial. Rethinking professionalism in early childhood: Untested feasibilities and critical ecologies. *Contemporary Issues in Early Childhood* 11 (1): 1–7. 2010.11.1.1.

Willer, B., A. Lutton & M. Ginsberg. 2011. The importance of early childhood teacher preparation: The perspectives and positions of the National Association for the Education of Young Children. In *The pre-k debates: Current controversies & issues*, eds. E. Zigler, W.S. Gilliam & W.S. Barnett, 77–83. Baltimore, MD: Brookes.